HOME: *A* CELEBRATION

THE BOOK OF THE HOMELESS EDITED BY EDITH WHARTON

HOME
A CELEBRATION

NOTABLE VOICES REFLECT ON THE MEANING OF HOME

Edited by CHARLOTTE MOSS

In collaboration with

 NO KID HUNGRY®

 RIZZOLI
NEW YORK

New York · Paris · London · Milan

CONTENTS

FOREWORD
By DARREN WALKER

A Hunger, and Home, for Justice

I
N 1916, Edith Wharton published *The Book of the Homeless*, an anthology of essays, poems, artworks, and musical scores from some of the most prominent, prolific creators of the time. The book arrived in the twilight of the Progressive Era, just months before the United States would join the First World War. As a renowned author and passionate supporter of the war effort, Wharton curated the compilation to raise funds for children displaced by the conflict. And she recruited a special contributor to draft a foreword to the collection: former President Theodore Roosevelt.

In his introduction, Roosevelt set the dire condition of these refugees in stark relief. He described the "harrowing tragedies" of children "driven from their country and on the verge of starvation, without food or shelter" and, indeed, "without hope."[1] Alas, he also described a reality that far too many children still face 105 years (and counting) later.

More than a century on, millions of children endure displacement and hunger. In the United States alone, one in every thirty children is homeless, while one in seven experiences hunger.[2] During the Covid-19 crisis, the situation has only grown worse; as of this writing, as many as one in six children could face hunger in 2021.

I grew up relatively poor, but for me, this kind of poverty is unimaginable. We always had enough—thanks to my mother, who worked as a nurse's aide—and I never had to wonder from where my next meal was coming. It's clear to me now that food in the cupboard and on the table was vital to my growth and success, as nutrition is for all children—and yet, for millions, this basic need remains unmet.

When a child goes hungry, every other area of their life suffers. Hunger impacts their social and educational development—their ability to learn, to connect with others, to dream. It affects their community, too. And if we trace childhood hunger back to its root causes, we find the vast inequities so many children and their families endure every day. Consider, for example, that 47 percent of American families have experienced hunger during our current global crisis, while the numbers are higher for Black (53 percent) and Latinx (56 percent) families. And nearly three-quarters of the parents dealing with food insecurity are essential workers, struggling to make their way from paycheck to paycheck.

In other words, hunger in the United States festers at the intersection of long-standing racial and economic disparities—and, worse, it exacerbates and perpetuates them.

In light of all this, my friend Charlotte Moss has compiled a collection for a new generation. Inspired by Wharton's *The Book of the Homeless*, Charlotte's *Home* brings together some of today's most influential artists and activists, cultural curators and producers. Joyce Carol Oates's iconic writing finds a place alongside Duro Olowu's innovative designs; Dan Barber's culinary genius melds seamlessly with Jon Meacham's insightful prose. And much like Wharton's project, this beautiful volume serves to raise both awareness and funds; the proceeds from *Home* will benefit children in need through No Kid Hungry, an extraordinary campaign committed to ending childhood hunger.

Of course, No Kid Hungry, a national campaign, is a vital service provider and part of the broader solution. They are already working with countless local organizations and school districts on the ground to help provide meals to students throughout the year. But ending childhood hunger will take more than one book or one organization.

We all share the responsibility to address the underlying issues that lead to childhood hunger in the first place: economic inequality, systemic racism and classism, unequal access to education, and the lack of affordable housing—to name just a few. As a country, we need to rebuild social safety nets, to better protect families in hard times, and to support economic policies and social programs—such as healthy school lunches—that set children and families up for success.

In the end, eradicating hunger will require that we support nonprofit campaigns such as No Kid Hungry while we also work to eliminate the circumstances which render such nonprofits overwhelmed during this season of Covid. It will require those of us included in this volume, and those who purchase it, to reflect on what we can do to address inequality in our society and ask if we have done enough.

So, as Edith Wharton's generous example inspired this project, and as you read these pages, I hope this volume encourages you to act for, even hunger for, justice.

1. publicdomainreview.org/collection/the-book-of-the-homeless-1916
2. air.org/center/national-center-family-homelessness

INTRODUCTION
By CHARLOTTE MOSS

*Y*EARS AGO, I obtained a copy of *The Book of the Homeless* edited by Edith Wharton in 1916, a fundraising effort she initiated to help refugees and children in Europe during the First World War. It was Wharton's idea to ask artists, writers, and poets to contribute an original piece, thereby generating great interest and, even more importantly, funds for the causes she was supporting. At this time Wharton had already written nine novels and would go on to become the first female Pulitzer Prize winner, in 1921. While living in France during the First World War, Wharton all but abandoned her writing. Instead, she opened workshops for women who had lost their jobs, founded American hostels sheltering more than four thousand five hundred Belgian and French refugees, and established the Children of Flanders Rescue Committee, which took care of over one thousand children.

Her literary success and influence allowed her to approach her good friend Henry James as well as Walter Gay, John Singer Sargent, Rupert Brooke, Thomas Hardy, Igor Stravinsky, W. B. Yeats, and fifty other writers and artists. In the first line of his introduction Theodore Roosevelt proclaimed, "It is not only a pleasure but a duty to write the introduction."

It is the concept of Wharton's book and the mention of duty that resonates now during the coronavirus crisis. In addition to more than half a million tragic deaths in the United States, millions of Americans have lost their jobs and their ability to pay bills, and cannot care for or feed their families. And many have been left homeless. It is the magnitude of this global crisis that moved me to adapt Wharton's goal for this book.

Home bears witness to the fact that philanthropy can be defined countless ways. Each contributor to this volume—artist, poet, photographer, historian, novelist, actor, and activist—has shared with us an interpretation of home, its meaning and importance in an individual life. Each has shared with us a personal account that streamed from head and heart through a pen, a brush, a laptop, or a camera lens.

Collectively, they represent the best of the American spirit. I hope that by their example they will empower and energize people everywhere to give something of themselves, to sacrifice something in order to help others. Philanthropy is an extension of heart—and *that* we all have. I am honored and overwhelmed that 122 generous spirits answered our calls, emails, and letters to come together in record time to enable us to feed children through No Kid Hungry, the beneficiary of this project. I am also equally honored that my publisher, Rizzoli, partnered with me on this effort to create *Home*.

My sitting room / study in New York includes a personal library of books and scrapbooks, a collection of fashion photography, and images of inspiring, creative, stylish women. Our collections define us; they ground us; they make our homes what they are.

PHOTOGRAPH BY PIETER ESTERSOHN

INTRODUCTION
By DEBBIE SHORE

Cofounder of Share Our Strength,
the organization behind No Kid Hungry

A S YOU HOLD THIS BOOK in your hands, I want you to know that you are sharing your strength. You are part of the solution to ending a problem that is impacting millions of children right here in the United States: *hunger.*

My brother Billy and I founded Share Our Strength together in 1984 in response to famine in Ethiopia. Core to our thinking from the very beginning was that everyone has a strength to share. We believed that if we provided people with an opportunity and a platform to get involved in fighting hunger, they would. With a $2,000 cash advance, we created Share Our Strength in a basement in Capitol Hill with the mission of eradicating hunger and poverty in the United States and abroad. Since then, Share Our Strength has been on the front lines of the war against poverty and hunger for more than thirty years, and through the work of our national campaign, No Kid Hungry—launched in 2010—we are not just fighting childhood hunger in America, but *ending* it. We have plenty of food and nutrition programs that work. The problem is that not enough kids have *access to* them. That's where we come in. No Kid Hungry works with schools, local nonprofits, and elected leaders to help launch and improve programs that give all kids the healthy food they need to thrive. Increasing participation in programs like school breakfast by making it part of the regular school day is just one example of how we've been able to make sure millions of kids are connected to food. A mission that has become much more dire in the wake of the coronavirus pandemic.

Before the pandemic, our country saw the lowest food insecurity rates since before the Great Recession of 2008—one in seven kids in America lived with hunger. Today that number has grown to as many as 13 million. This drastic change in such a short time period revealed that many families were just one lost job, health crisis, or stalled school meal program away from hunger. Hunger in America can take different forms. It's a mom who skips a meal so her child can eat. It's the parent who has to make the unthinkable choice between paying for groceries or paying the rent. But it doesn't need to be this way. Childhood hunger is a solvable problem, and we will work even harder in the pandemic's recovery to end it. From our work on the ground with schools and local organizations, ensuring they have the investment funds and resources they need—refrigeration units to transportation vehicles and more—to reach kids with food no matter where they are learning. To Capitol Hill, where we're advocating for strong policies to strengthen nutrition programs like SNAP that help feed more families. But as we continue this fight, this work isn't possible without your strength to share.

Supporters share their work in so many ways. CEOs engage their employees, customers, and investors in campaigns that generate donations; celebrities share important information with fans and generate awareness of childhood hunger; chefs cook meals for fundraising dinners and have helped provide free meals for communities during the pandemic. Tens of thousands of people simply give what they can spare. And you, by holding this book in your hands, by choosing to make this purchase, are providing funds to help ensure that millions of children across the country are connected to food. And families no longer have to make unthinkable choices to put food on the table.

As you read through these pages, reflect on what "home" means to you. "Home," to me, means family and food. Home is a reflection of me and my daughter, Sofie. A place where Sofie's artwork, from the doodles at age four to the inspiring oil paintings at age seventeen, covers many walls. Home is where I spend weekends planning a menu, readying the kitchen and chopping, roasting, seeding, blending, tasting. Home is where I raised my daughter; just me and my girl taking on the world. Home will always be synonymous with her. It is a place, but it's also a feeling of warmth and safety, sometimes quiet, sometimes noisy, but always providing a soft landing and an invitation to be my authentic self.

Everyone deserves to feel this way and your support is helping to make a difference for millions of kids. And for families, who are at the heart of any "home."

Thank you to Charlotte Moss, Rizzoli New York, and our amazing donors who have supported this project and continue sharing their strengths to make no kid hungry a reality!

NO KID HUNGRY

No child should go hungry in America. But in 2021, one in six kids could face hunger. No Kid Hungry is working to end childhood hunger by helping launch and improve programs that give all kids the healthy food they need to thrive. No Kid Hungry works to eliminate any barriers that stand in the way of a child having access to food. No Kid Hungry supports programs like school meals, food banks, and other community groups feeding kids, and pushes for legislation to help feed more kids.

This is a problem we know how to solve. Through a combination of emergency grants, strategic assistance, advocacy, and awareness, No Kid Hungry is equipping communities across the country with the resources they need. No Kid Hungry has a plan to make sure children are fed, both during this crisis and every day. You can help. No Kid Hungry is a campaign of Share Our Strength, an organization committed to ending hunger and poverty. Join us at NoKidHungry.org.

UMBERTO PASTI

The Cave

As a child I was building huts all the time. In the trees, with a piece of cardboard and a couple of planks laid among the branches. And in my bed, with blankets and sheets, and pillows for walls and a stool in the middle to support the roof. At twelve I had a room to myself. Since then I have changed into a mammal who must bring everything he needs into his den, in order to survive a perpetual winter. I used to sleep and study surrounded by the things I couldn't do without: rocks, roots, piles of old tin cans, stacks of books and newspapers, bowls full of quartz eggs, a railroad, seashells, some wax fruits my grandmother gave me, small Indian elephants, the birdcage with my wooden Aztec priests stuck with plasticine to swings, and perches of deceased canaries. I realized that at this pace, in a couple of years, I would no longer be able to reach the bed. I had to get rid of the junk. I became a collector.

I decided to confine myself only to prewar toys, fossils, minerals, and the headgear and feathered items made by "primitive" peoples; then, tentatively at first and gradually with greater confidence, I devoted myself to the masks and fetishes of Africa and Oceania, first editions of Italian poetry, Islamic tiles, pieces of carpeting and fabrics. After almost forty years I am still there: to my primary necessities I have added the painted furniture of the Berbers of northern Morocco, folk earthenware, and whalebones. My idea of home, now that I have three houses and no longer live in a single room, is still the same: my hut from back then, which is what all my rooms put together amount to, ideally. I don't care about stocks of water and food, or if my drawers are full of towels and sheets (but I care dearly for my hundreds of plates, and dozens of old blankets): the objects I really can't do without are my chosen family, saved from the diaspora of life and finally reunited, sitting next to one another, back from the din of Babel and finally having a nice chat all together. Thanks to them I live in a close weave of whispers and words, soft as the finest pashmina, which welcomes and comforts me.

It's strange that a man like me, who lives a lot in the open air, has this need of protection. But sometimes the words that trees and clouds say to each other, and the violet outline of the hills and the horizon on which they fade are so sharp they scare me, so poignant they make me weep. This is why I plunge into shrubs and hide. To stop trembling, to stop weeping, I carve out my flower beds in the boundless land. I need huts. I have no love for the houses of others, I feel uncomfortable, I don't understand the language. And I hate the metallic vocabulary of hotels. But once, walking in a forest, I met a shepherd. He was in rags, with long dirty nails and tufts of beard. He invited me to have tea. He lived in a cave. The ground was soft with dried ferns and in a corner there was a fireplace. He had been living there for twenty years; he had left the village because there was too much noise, too much noise—he'd made a desperate grunt, covering his ears with his hands, before suddenly flashing me a radiant, toothless smile of complicity. The water began to boil. Perhaps it was the slanting sunrays playing on his tattered army blanket, or the glinting jam jar in which he kept honey stolen from the combs, or the polished words spoken by some hare bones by the fire . . . I fell asleep. The air, which smelled like hay and feet, brimmed with all the nice conversations that since my childhood can be heard in my hut.

PHOTOGRAPH BY SIMON WATSON

ADDIE CHAPIN

maine

I walk down a path one morning in Maine lined with Christmas trees
The shore is not yet, but I will take a bet
I can smell the sound of the Seas

Up through the clearing, the Ocean is nearing; a vast and quiet debut
Will put all to rest, draw near to Her chest
Let the waves wash over you, too

What does the bee see? Does he see what I see, deerfooting in the sand
The tracks are all there; where they go, don't know where
A rising tide they won't withstand

What does the deer hear, does she hear what I hear, caw-cawing above the shore
I see it's the bird, always true to its word
Till one day it won't caw no more

What does the gull mull? Does it mull the other gull skull, half eaten among the shells?
How did it end? At the hand of a friend
Or in glory by ocean swells

In the end we're all here, Bird and Bee, Deer and Man, drawing nigh to rocky Sea
It holds Life, it holds Death, it holds all of us now
In dear old Vacationland.

TOMALES POINT, 2020
MIXED MEDIA ON CANVAS

Home is a place where it's safe to fall apart and come back together again. A place to be exactly who you are, in whichever season or state you may find yourself. Nature, and specifically the trails of Point Reyes, has provided for me an incredible sense of peace. A place to keep moving, and be still, all at the same time. A healing all its own.

JOHN DERIAN

I find real joy and peace in the home I share with Stephen Kent Johnson in Provincetown, Massachusetts. The house was built in 1789 for a sea captain (Captain Small) and came with exposed horsehair and seashell plaster walls, some intact vintage wallpapers, and colorful splattered floors. Basically "move in ready."

Besides the pelargoniums blooming year round all over the west side of the house, we like to celebrate the seasons with flowers from our garden and foraged by our friend and gardener, Tim Callis.

AL ROKER

WHAT IS HOME? What does it mean to you? Those are interesting questions, ones that we don't always think about. The answers can be as varied as the people answering them. For many of us, it's either an automatic response or one that we take for granted.

For me, home means family. Growing up, our family lived in an apartment until my parents scraped together the down payment for a semidetached house on a quarter acre lot on a corner in St. Albans, Queens. It was the point of immense pride for my family; a piece of the American Dream. Never mind there were six kids and two adults sharing three bedrooms and one bathroom. It was ours. It's why I am so punctual. You follow a strict bathroom schedule when there are eight people sharing one bathroom.

During this pandemic, for many, home has become a school, a cafeteria, an office, a rec center, and any other number of multipurpose places as we hunker down, and venture out only occasionally, trying to find some normalcy in our lives.

I love being home. This pandemic has made me appreciate the blessings of being able to quarantine at home. It makes me look at my home in a whole new light. I can enjoy the different spaces that I take for granted, as my family and I look for spots to gather and to find a little personal time.

We spend so much time scurrying to and from work, meetings, activities, and festivities, our homes become way stations where we eat, sleep, and head out again. But since March of 2020, we have been able to really linger where we live. We have time to connect with one another. Some might say we have a little too much time to connect. And we've been able to watch what has been happening in our country and take in these momentous events. A lot of folks have seen a lot and have been moved to action, and we have watched that unfold as well.

For too many Americans, this sheltering in place is an unattainable luxury. Something that many of us take for granted, others can only dream about. Would that they could complain about being "stuck" at home during the pandemic. Unfortunately, for an unacceptable number of Americans, struggling to maintain a home and put food on the table is an "either/or" proposition and the possibility of staying home isn't an option. These folks work at stocking shelves, delivering our Amazon products, and keeping our infrastructure and safety services going so we have the ability to enjoy our homes.

That's what the questions "What is home?" and "What does it mean to you?" conjure up. To me home means so much, but to those without one, it means even more.

MARC APPLETON

Home is where the heart is, and the heart
is where we say that love abides,
surprised by something beautiful that hides
in secret ambush from a world apart.

DOUGLAS FRIEDMAN

Home, as a concept, has evolved for me over the years as I spend less and less time in one, in the traditional sense. My work keeps me on the road most of the time, and I have learned to make home the place where I am at that very moment . . . so it's less about the physical space for me, and more about the feeling, the emotion of "home." And that feeling is built around the house I spent ten years creating, deep in the desert of West Texas.

JOYCE CAROL OATES

HOUSE   HOME   HOUSE

HOUSE is the labyrinth at the center of which HOME is secreted.

HOUSE is visible from a distance, HOME is the invisible within.

HOUSE is emptiness waiting to be filled by HOME.

HOUSE contains HOME but is not identical with HOME.

HOUSE darkens as the sun wanes. HOME brightens with interior lights.

HOUSE is body, HOME indwelling spirit.

HOUSE FOR SALE is a frequent sign. HOME FOR SALE, never.

HOUSE has a market price. HOME, never.

HOUSE is measurements, HOME immeasurable.

HOUSE is an entity in three dimensions: brick, mortar, redwood, glass, shingleboard, poured concrete.
     HOME is breath.

Many HOUSES. A single HOME.

HOUSES, interchangeable. HOMES, never.

HOUSE is the place where memories are secreted. HOME is memories.

HOME, happiness of HOUSE.

HOME, soul of HOUSE.

HOME is the uplifted face, joy in kissing in foolish happiness and being kissed.

HOME is soft-falling snow, HOUSE is shelter beneath the snow.

Across 5,000 miles, HOME exerts its unerring spell.

HOUSE has too many rooms, no one has counted them. HOME is a single room dazzled by light.

HOUSE echoes with emptiness. HOME with voices.

On shelves of the HOUSE, accumulations of HOME.

HOME is the music, HOUSE the instrument upon which music is possible.

Where cats nap luxuriant in a patch of sunshine on a carpet, that is HOME.

Where the beloved is, that is HOME.

Where the beloved is no longer, that is HOUSE.

For HOUSE will prevail after HOME has vanished as the scattered bones of a singular skeleton
     will prevail in the chaos of soil.

HOME is the place where the ashes of the dead accumulate.

HOME is the place where, when you seek him, the husband lifts his face to be kissed.

HOME is what you seek when you enter HOUSE making your anxious way through the rooms.

Hello? Where are you?—a cry echoes through the rooms.

It's me. I'm home. Darling? Where are you?

HOUSE never dreams. HOME is dreams.

The place where the bereft drift like ghosts seeking ghosts, that is HOME.

The place where shelves of books have commingled, that is HOME.

Where HOME has departed, HOUSE remains.

In the HOUSE, HOME is shrinking. Each day an earlier dusk. One by one windows are shuttered.
    Rooms are shut off.

How fragile, HOME. For HOUSE will outlive HOME.

Hurrying upstairs in the HOUSE, astonished to see that the husband's bedroom is empty.

From no window of the HOUSE is the husband visible outside. Yet, you move eagerly from
    one window to another.

Because the husband is in none of the rooms of HOME, the husband abides everywhere and anywhere.

HOME is closets in which the clothes of the beloved dead hang in readiness for their return.

As HOME fades from HOUSE, a stark beauty emerges.

HOME is lost to you, you will become a wanderer.

You will think—*But what has happened to me? Is this what I have become?*

His being has expanded to fit all of the universe.

Where there is no boundary, the center is everywhere.

This place where he *was*, a place that (once) contained him, now not HOME but a memory of HOME.

I have failed you as a husband, by dying.

If HOUSE could dream, HOUSE would dream HOME.

Where *was* is, *is* once was.

HOME was, HOUSE is.

Since the vanishing of the husband HOME has begun to fade.

HOME is where, in his closets, nothing will be altered.

Hurrying into the husband's study to greet him with a kiss but halted midway like a doe shot
    in mid-leap for the room is (still) empty. . .

Mystery here that the worn leather chair so many years occupied is empty. . .

How HOUSE is haunted by HOME.

How HOUSE is rooms, walls, floors and ceilings, staircases, windows from which HOME has faded.

Bright sunlight, mists, pelting rain, lightly falling snow—mistakenly believed to be,
    because *now,* permanent.

Warmth has departed from his hands, like his old strength. Yet these are *his* hands, eagerly you seize them.

Begging the husband—*I don't want to live without you.*

The rebuke of the husband—*If you love me, you will outlive me.*

HOME is the place of memory. Soon, all that will remain of HOME will be memory.

How silent, HOUSE! No vocabulary.

In the HOUSE, rooms that cannot be entered.

Where the dead abide soft-crackling underfoot like the husks of winged insects, that is HOME.

Where no new snapshots will be thumb-tacked to the cork bulletin board, that is HOME.

HOME that is lost, is lost forever.

Not a ferocious gale, a slow leak like air from a failing lung.

Since the husband has departed the husband can be anywhere. The husband can be everywhere.
    The husband has said—*The human brain is infinite. Only where we inhabit is finite.*

RACHAEL RAY

What home means to me has changed many times. I make a home in New York City, but the Adirondacks is where I've lived since I was in second grade. Home is a state of mind and heart. I am a homemaker, and wherever we call home, the place I feel the most comfort is in my kitchen.

TUNA CASSEROLE
Serves 4

Just the other day, I was looking through the pantry, pulling things out and trying to comfort my family and myself by cooking a simple dinner. I made my version of an American classic: tuna casserole. My sister does not eat tuna, so I made a separate casserole with leftover rotisserie chicken—same time, two different pans. To make the version with chicken, omit the mushrooms and add 1 small peeled and chopped carrot and ½ cup peas. Instead of the tuna, use 2 ½ to 3 cups chopped rotisserie or poached chicken.

- 1 12-ounce package extra-wide egg noodles
- Kosher salt
- 5 tablespoons butter
- 7 to 8 mushrooms, such as cremini or white, cleaned and quartered
- 2 large shallots or 1 small yellow onion, finely chopped
- 1 small leek, trimmed, cleaned, quartered, and thinly sliced
- 1 celery stalk, finely chopped with leafy tops
- 2 cloves garlic, finely chopped or grated
- 2 tablespoons fresh thyme leaves, stripped from the stem, or 2 teaspoons dried thyme
- Freshly ground white or black pepper
- 4 tablespoons all-purpose flour

- ⅓ cup dry sherry
- 1 cup chicken bone broth, regular broth, or stock
- 1 cup milk
- ½ cup heavy cream (can substitute 1 ½ cups half and half for the milk and cream)
- Freshly grated nutmeg
- 1 ½ to 1 ¾ cups grated Parmigiano-Reggiano cheese
- 2 (5-ounce) cans solid white wild- or line-caught tuna in water, no salt added, drained and coarsely flaked
- 2 teaspoons fresh lemon juice, from ½ lemon
- 1 cup crushed parmesan-flavored crackers, breadcrumbs, or crushed saltines
- ¼ cup combination of flat-leaf parsley and leafy green celery tops, chopped

Set an oven rack in the center of the oven and preheat to 375°F.

Bring a large pot of water to a boil for the egg noodles. Salt the boiling water and cook the egg noodles 1 to 2 minutes shy of the package instructions. Drain and set aside until you are ready to toss with the casserole mixture.

While the egg noodles cook, place a large skillet over medium heat and melt the butter. Add the mushrooms and cook for 2 to 3 minutes, then add the shallots, leek, celery, garlic, and thyme. Season the mixture with salt and pepper and let cook until the vegetables are tender, 4 to 5 minutes. Sprinkle the mixture with the flour and stir to incorporate and cook out the floury taste, 1 to 2 minutes more. Add the sherry and stir, then add the bone broth, milk, and heavy cream. Add a few grates of fresh nutmeg and bring to a simmer. Let cook until the mixture is slightly thickened, a few minutes more. Turn the heat to low, add ½ to ¾ cup of the Parmigiano while stirring, then gently fold in the tuna and lemon juice. Add the cooked egg noodles and gently stir to combine. Transfer the mixture to a large casserole dish.

In a small bowl, blend the remaining 1 cup Parmigiano, the crushed crackers, and chopped parsley and celery tops. Top the casserole with this mixture.

Bake until the top is light brown and the casserole is bubbling, 7 to 8 minutes.

TORY BURCH

Home is a place for people to come and go, filled with love and family, somewhere that is lived in and never too perfect. Everything has a memory tied to it and every room represents different times and places in my life. I had the most extraordinary childhood growing up on our farm in Valley Forge. My mom is still the most incredible hostess and was known for her extraordinary dinner parties but what I loved most: she spent the same amount of time and effort on a family dinner.

AMY ASTLEY

*T*HE ROOMS THAT EMBRACE US and the people we love are so much more than just places to live. Modest or opulent, temporary or ancestral, their walls encourage us to put down roots, to devise environments that not only please the eye but also comfort and soothe. This is especially true when times are challenging or when circumstances seem uncertain, whether one is a child or an adult. As sculptor Louise Bourgeois explained to *Architectural Digest*, her own home proved to be "my defense against the open road, the open world where you are likely to get pushed around." Her words, like those of other soul-searching homeowners that have appeared in *AD*'s pages over the last hundred-plus years, resonate, reminding us that there is more to a room than beautiful things comfortably arranged. The best ones are rich with secrets and footnotes, allusions, hopes, and desires.

"This house tells a good story. Or it will tell a good story," Shonda Rhimes, the producer and screenwriter, told *AD* of her long but successful search for the perfect place for her and her family, adding, "My girls will grow up here, become women here. Life will happen here. Laughter will happen here. Love will live here." Poet Maya Angelou echoed that observation in an unexpectedly moving essay about how the right house, discovered after years of personal turmoil, calmed her soul and grounded her emotions. "Because it is my home, not only have I found myself healed of the pain of a broken love affair," she candidly admitted, "but I find that rejection slips from publishers do not hurt so badly."

The more essential a house is to one's identity, the more its rooms embody ourselves over time. Color, art, objects, furnishings, and textiles—or, on the other hand, the lack thereof—coalesce into an autobiography of who we are at any given moment in time and, just as importantly, who we may be becoming. "It is the spirit you fill it with that is important," painter David Hockney has said, while mixed-media artist Ugo Rondinone has observed that he looked forward to how his relatively spare country place "will continue to grow and evolve." That sentiment is shared by interior designer Markham Roberts and dealer James Sansum, the former saying, "This house is something we've been involved with for nearly twenty years now. We're still working on it."

To accept that the place you live, like the people who live in it, will always remain unfinished, is a condition that the novelist James Baldwin saw as hopeful, even perhaps the whole point. "There is always something in need of repair or renewal or burial," he wrote of his old farmhouse. "But this exasperating rigor is good for the soul, for it means that one can never suppose one's work is done."

Interior designer Markham Roberts and James Sansum's living room at their
getaway on Puget Sound in Washington State.

PHOTOGRAPH BY NELSON HANCOCK

CANDICE BERGEN

My daughter encouraged me to paint after her friends liked a tote bag I had decorated for her. The result was Bergenbags: I painted Vuitton or Hermès tote bags for friends and strangers and gave the proceeds to charity. After painting around a hundred bags and covering every table in our apartment with painted tote bags, I moved back to taking paying jobs where I kept the money. I never studied painting and learned the little I know in the doing. It is an extremely pleasant way to pass the morning with a little Bobby Darin playing. Very soothing and meditative. I recommend it!

ANN ZIFF

*T*HE POWER OF THE ARTS TO INSPIRE, to elevate the human spirit, and to heal is something I have spent a good part of my life discovering and supporting. The need for that healing force has never been greater than at this historically challenging moment.

By way of background, my mother was an opera singer who performed in Europe and on the Metropolitan Opera stage, so I was raised with a love of this special art form and a love of all kinds of music and performance art. I received a master's degree in psychiatric social work in my twenties from New York University, where I had focused my studies on the ways the performing arts could play a part in the healing process for those suffering from chronic and emotional illnesses. More than forty years later I completed my second master's, in Music Therapy at Temple University.

As chairman of the Metropolitan Opera, and vice chair of Lincoln Center for the Performing Arts, for the last twenty-five years I've devoted my time and resources to the remarkable benefits that music and the arts bring to all levels of society. I am a founding board member of Sing For Hope (SFH), a charitable organization whose mission is to bring the performing arts to schools, hospitals, nursing homes, and those in underserved communities in New York City. I have been inspired by all the performing artists who have devoted their time and creative energy to sharing the benefits of the arts with those who might not otherwise be able to enjoy them. For one program, SFH invites artists to design themed pianos that are then placed in public areas throughout the boroughs of New York City. To watch the joy on the faces of people who have never played a piano before or to recognize a song, or just enjoy a beautiful moment in a hectic and often downtrodden environment is more than soul satisfying. Yes, it's important to contribute dollars, but when you don't have the financial capability to donate large sums, every bit counts. And every hour you spend helping with your time and talent counts in equal measure.

Our country and our world are desperate for relief from the anxiety and stress we have all experienced this year. Although we have not been able to enjoy gathering for live performances, the artists among us have not been silenced. Musicians, singers, actors, and dancers have performed in their homes, or on street corners, or in vacant lots. But they all have suffered enormous setbacks in seclusion. The organizations that provide the tools and support for these artists to stay on their chosen course need our assistance now more than ever. It is only through the generosity of donors and patrons of the arts and education that these artists will survive on their chosen path. We must continue to support their dreams and their future.

The ~~steaming woods think it queer~~

To ~~village~~ ^hove ^must

The ~~horse~~ ~~begins~~ ^to think it queer

~~To~~ ^To Stop with not a farm house near

Between a ~~forest and~~ ^the woods an afrozen a lake

The darkest evening of the year

~~He~~ ^She .. ^her gives harness bells a shake

To ask if there is some mistake

The only other sounds ^the sweep

Of easy wind and ~~falling~~ ^downy flake.

The woods are lovely dark and deep

But I have promises to keep

~~That ~~ ^no ~~And there are miles~~ ~~the woods a shade~~

And miles to go before I sleep

And miles to go before I sleep

ANNIE LEIBOVITZ

LEFT: Jones Library, Amherst, Massachusetts

ABOVE: Dad's 1988 Oldsmobile Station Wagon, Upstate New York

BIANCA JAGGER

Nature is home to me; that is why I love this beautiful mulberry tree.

ANNIE SCHLECHTER

I was lucky to grow up in
a home of color, books & humor. Every year since I
was a child, I made a calendar for my parents.
These photos of their home come from one such calendar.

WILLIAM CURTIS

Salmagundi Luncheon is a watercolor painting
of an intimate corner in the dining room
of the Salmagundi Club in New York City.
The painting is an image that anticipates the
ritual experience of the meal. The scene
evidences architectural elements that comple-
ment the purpose of dining and homelike
social interaction. Its light-filled character
evidences the room's (*home's*) connection with
the world through the leaded glass.

PHOTOGRAPHS BY FRANÇOIS HALARD

DAVID NETTO

Notes on Home: A Visit to Betty and François Catroux in Provence, May 2015
DEDICATED TO THE MEMORY OF FRANÇOIS CATROUX, 1936–2020

ETTY'S PERSONAL STYLE has evolved into a fairly consistent and disciplined rock 'n' roll aesthetic with a great emphasis on black, specifically black leather and puffer jackets over black pencil jeans. It is the sort of uniform Betty knows is an antidote to age, à la Lagerfeld and Hedi Slimane—someone so fearless-looking is always the youngest in the room. At all times arresting and unique in her physical appearance, which thanks to her strong jaw and boyish frame evoke an androgyne beauty, or even that of an animal (sometimes it is striking in photographs how much she resembles a young deer), today she might be taken for a missing blonde member of The Ramones.

Intimately connected as a couple, at home in a marriage that perhaps has seen many tests—and for sure survived them all—they have grown closer with time. How many people among the Beau Monde can you say that about? Betty, famously the muse of many talents, is completely outspoken and convinced on the subject of the importance of her husband's gifts. She does not throw around the word "genius" or bestow it lightly, but she refers to François as that. What they don't like to do is talk about style or analyze it too much, but in their personal outlook and in their own houses in Paris and Provence they now share a commitment to something very hard to do with style unless you already know how to do everything else: an elegant plainness.

The later work of Catroux reflects this sensibility, projects that identify a trend toward lightness and editing within Catroux's "voice" in design. By saying so much about his personal life I hope to shed some light upon a source of its style—his marriage, the sense of home he shares with Betty, and the place they are happiest.

François and Betty's favorite place to spend time today is Les Ramades, the country retreat fashioned from a sixteenth-century farmhouse they have owned since 1990 in the Provençal village of Lourmarin. They travel relentlessly but look forward to spending holidays and long weekends there, as well as the traditional French vacation month of August. Provence can be a very social place, particularly in summer, but that is not what this couple is here for. François is a lifelong sports car aficionado and likes to drive his Aston Martin at genuinely alarming speeds on the narrow country roads. Betty—who refuses to ride in what she condemns as a "naff" and vulgar machine—thinks of anything *but* fashion and decoration, two subjects in which she has no interest but upon which she has had such a profound, even historic, effect. She contemplates a memoir of her relationship with Yves Saint Laurent and the times they shared, which she may decide to write—or may not. A private person with enough living behind her to quell any fear she might miss something by staying home, she dances, swims, loves to drink Sauternes.

François runs the house, protects his wife from invitations she would rather not accept, and makes the arrangements to have dinner put on the table by an elegant couple who have worked for them for many years. He is a very hands-on gardener, and will make with pleasure a long trip across the Provençal countryside to visit a plant nursery if he has heard a beautiful tree may be available. At Les Ramades the atmosphere is privileged but also cozy, and one can see something defining the life in this house, which is rarer than it should be: its owners are truly *at home*.

ALEX BEARD

ON CAMEL SAFARI, 2016
INK ON PAPER

This work was created in Kenya, a place that I consider my second *home*.

ANTHONY S. BARNES

THE WERF AT BABYLONSTOREN, 2020
WATERCOLOR ON PAPER

This is a scene from an old wine farm in South Africa called Babylonstoren.
   These old Cape homesteads are made of simple, local materials: sun-dried mud bricks, covered in lime plaster and lime-wash, roofed with thatch, cut from local wetlands. Something so classic, simple, and rooted about them.
   I have lived in the United States since 1981 and love and cherish my new home, my long-held US citizenship and passport. But South Africa is the country I am originally from.

KIM McCARTY

2 BLUE OWLS, 2017
WATERCOLOR ON PAPER

Every midnight in the spring of 2020, when the world was adjusting
to the pandemic, I heard barn owls hooting from the tree next to
my bedroom window. The familiar cries brought a sense of solace
to an agitated sleep and made life feel almost normal.

Alice & Fanny's Victory Garden Lettuce & Herb Salad

Pick several handfuls of garden lettuces & a bunch each of parsley & chervil. Wash your lettuce & herbs gently in plenty of water & roll in cloth towels to dry. Pluck the leaves from your herbs.

Place all your lettuces & herbs in a beautiful bowl and dress with garlicky vindigrette: pound 1 garlic clove with a pinch of salt add a splash of red wine vinegar and let sit a moment. Whisk in a glug of good olive oil. Taste! Tweak! Dress!

CHIP KIDD

BETWEEN HEAVEN AND HELL

In 2011, when we bought our apartment in Palm Beach (above, detail), we treated it as a blank canvas, and I tried to think about decorating it less as an interior and more as an art project. I really needed this creative 180, I needed a break from ink on paper. As a graphic designer with an emphasis on book covers, over the years I've found myself correcting people when they refer to me as an artist. "No," I would say, "an artist is someone who makes something you hang on the wall. I make something you wrap around a book." And I still say it. But, I had often wondered what it would be like to dip a toe into that frame of mind (mixed metaphors!), and the new place had plenty of what I don't have in New York City: blank wall space.

So I thought about all the book jackets I'd done since 1987 (there are a lot of them), and about which ones might work as, well, art. The two you see above have special meaning to me. On the left is one of the last covers I designed for my (now late) husband, the poet J. D. McClatchy. It's actually an image of someone caught in a sail during the America's Cup race (don't ask me what year). On the right is my favorite jacket I did for Cormac McCarthy. It's meant to represent the relentless serial killer who haunts the novel, but it's really a stock photo of some guy out for a jog in the sunset.

Formally, these two complemented each other, even though they were designed well over two decades apart. And then, once they were on the wall, it struck me: they seemed to represent Paradise vs. Eternal Damnation. But which one was which?

ROBERT RUFINO

It's a joy to come home knowing that your best friend will always be there to greet you. It's sometimes less fun to see what mischief they have gotten into!

Like an old married couple, we begin to look alike. This is Windsor at my desk, imitating me. The feeling of joy and love we get from our animal companions is priceless.

PHOTOGRAPH BY JEFF HIRSCH

ANDREW SOLOMON

Country Life

WE SPENT TEN YEARS renovating and restoring our country house in Rhinebeck (corrupt builders, hidden conditions, the town zoning board) and we moved in, officially, in late 2018. There is little I loathe more than moving: the boxes were everywhere, the good offices of our beleaguered cleaning ladies seemed barely to clear the dust, there were no curtains, the furniture was either missing or not yet reupholstered, the plumbing made inexplicable shrieking noises, and the phones rang even when no one was calling. The yard was strewn with outdoor furniture that had not yet found its place, giving the impression that we were hoping to be cast in a remake of *The Beverly Hillbillies*. The books! Box upon box upon box. Getting the books on the shelves in any kind of coherent order was a project that demanded only a month or so of full-time attention, and who doesn't have a month to while away in such a rewarding pursuit? Things we hated awaited wall space (why did we ever frame that?) and things we loved were impossible to hang. The hot water was so hot that you could burn yourself if you turned the faucet wrong. The Internet came and went like a poltergeist, and the oven could be set only to raw or burnt. Our odd-sized bed had no sheets that fit, so we were camping out in a guest room without good lamps, leaving us with flashlights balanced on our knees for reading stories to our son George, then nine. Cumbersome things neither my husband John nor I remembered purchasing had been delivered to our house, and our favorite Regency settee had vanished along with the German baroque cradle John gave me the year we agreed to have a child. We had bemoaned the costs of construction terminable and interminable and celebrated being done with it, but somehow as we moved in, we incurred a panoply of peculiar bills that would have daunted the Sultan of Brunei.

In addition, there was a human cost to calculate: things I loved because they had belonged to my grandmother offended John's aesthetic, while things he loved because they had belonged to his grandmother required of me a tact I had seldom deployed in our twenty years together. He had bought things he knew I wouldn't like and then given them to me as presents so that I had to live with them. I had bought things I knew he might not like and then daringly positioned them where I thought he would accede to their display. I rearranged about half the things he objected to, and he caved on about half the things I objected to. I gave John a drawing as an anniversary gift that he correctly observed would look best in my study, where it now hangs—in the end, then, a present to myself. All marriages have their politics and ours had been fairly benign; now, we seemed to burst with arguments both suppressed and expressed. I pride myself on my intellect and humanitarianism, but I never forget that my first serious boyfriend and I broke up over our differing opinions about the curtains in a hotel in Sintra. Maps of Portugal still make me sad.

Moving in was far more gradual than we had anticipated. John vehemently took on the picture-hanging, rather to my irritation, then proved gifted at it, rather to my surprise. I ran the show on the pelmets since I'm the pelmet enthusiast in our family (every family should have one). I ordered all the dog beds and most of the lampshades. We had of course been in negotiations like this since the first designs were proposed for the house by our beloved friend and trusted designer Robert Couturier, whom I had known for thirty years and who had been our stalwart through the interminable construction process. Robert functioned as a visionary therapist, proposing alternate solutions whenever John and I were fixated on opposing strategies. I could tell when Robert was pretending to agree with John for the sake of peace, but I could never tell when he was pretending to agree with me. I mostly agreed with Robert; doing so made life easier and his taste ultimately accorded with my own. But there were frustrating inefficiencies in the process. I tried to wheedle and beguile out of his office the fundamental decorative items we so clearly needed, then occasionally got all dramatic and peevish until, bit by bit, things began to show up. I occasionally got dramatic and peevish with John, too, and so did he with me. George watched all this neurotic conflict in a state of bewilderment. He had seen us agree on so many direly important things and now there was a basso continuo of passive aggression thrumming under our happy family.

The first year in a new house is always experimental, but by Christmas of 2019, we had resolved many of the most pressing issues and I had ceased to regret that we ever contemplated a house in the country. We passed some pleasant winter weekends in Rhinebeck and drank champagne in front of the fire. The phones no longer rang at all, most of the rooms felt unfinished but habitable, and my beloved research assistant had dealt with the books. The lighting was all wrong in most of the rooms but we at least knew how we wanted to fix it. The pot rack! Well, one can live without a pot rack for a while if the beleaguered man who is making it does gorgeous metalwork on a fitful basis. I finally had the family photos all printed to the right sizes for the nineteenth-century frames I had collected and out they went on the big console tables in the living room. They made the house feel like ours—at least, they made it feel that way to me.

When George's spring break, 2020, rolled around, we headed off for a week in the tropics with my extended family, only to depart early because the border was being sealed. Upon our return, we drove from the airport to Rhinebeck and moved temporarily into living permanently in what we'd imagined to be a weekend house. As the Covid months wore on, the place took on the feeling that places have only when they are genuinely inhabited, the character no house has unless its owners can find their way through it in the dark. We were no longer perched there like birds ready to take wing with a change of the wind. We burrowed in like moles. I had always been a city boy, born and bred in New York and later an inhabitant of London, of Moscow, of big, busy metropolises where everything was happening at once. John joked that my idea of appreciating the countryside was looking out the window at sunset through the bottom of a wine glass. But now there were no cities: New York as we'd known it was erased. While isolation would have felt sinister in Manhattan, it felt appropriate in Rhinebeck.

I was overwhelmed with gratitude that this twelve-years-by-then project had come to fruition in time for us to retreat there and was perhaps grateful also that it hadn't been ready sooner, that we were still discovering the thrill of residence, which made our sequestration feel more like an adventure and less like a prison sentence. Unlike many of my friends, I could go out for walks any time and without a mask; I could take George to the trampoline; I could eat on the loggia. John had planted a vegetable garden and we had tomatoes so sweet they might have been nectarines. It is true that I sometimes felt like a B-movie Marie Antoinette in this rural idyll—frankly, I would have gone for a flock of sheep and an outfit designed for appearing to herd them—but the first order of business was to remain cheerful, and we mostly did.

I arrived at material obsessions to distract me from the fact that we might all die soon from a deadly virus that had already snuffed out people I knew, leaving us quietly bereft. When I couldn't cope with reports of refrigerated trucks full of corpses, I measured for the missing lampshades. When I was working on my book and failed to persuade the words to come, I went online looking for antique tapestry cushions. When I felt that the intensity of sheltering with my husband, my son, and my surrogate father-in-law was more than I could bear, I rearranged the dishes so that they had sensible permanent locations. And when the fact that Donald Trump was president struck terror and outrage into my soul, I figured out where we could best deploy the Chinese Chippendale table (which was definitely not Chinese and probably not Chippendale, though it was, at least, a table).

This whole line of behavior drove our son wild with irritation. George is boyish to an extent that seems almost embarrassing to gay parents. He would happily wear the same t-shirt and nylon shorts (where on earth did the nylon shorts even come from?) every day and wouldn't brush his hair for a month at a time. He likes his comforts and wants the bed to be yielding and the pillows to be soft, but whether the linens are trimmed in the same color as the upholstered box spring is a matter to which he refused attention even after it was delineated to him a dozen triumphant times. He liked good restaurants when one could still go to them and he is a food snob, turning up his nose at overcooked fish or doughy pizza, but whether he is served on Spode, Meissen, Flora Danica, or paper plates is a matter of sheer indifference to him. He knows our house to be beautiful more than he perceives it to be beautiful and he doesn't much care either way.

I had been working for months on an article about polygamy and polyamory, the details of which I thought as interesting a topic as any other available one, given that none of us was doing anything but that (me), George's schoolwork (him—and he definitely did not want to discuss it at dinner), and planting things (John). So I often shared information about my day's progress on Utah fundamentalism. George, thoroughly exasperated, finally said, "Daddy, don't you ever talk about anything besides Mormons and curtains?"

CAROLINE WEBER

Home Like Love
After W. H. Auden

Home, say the architects, is a space:
A structure defined by ceilings and walls,
Doorways and windows, stairways and halls,
Home above all is a physical place.

The builders point out that it's steel, planks, and brick,
With bolts, nails, and mortar to make it all stick.
(The Three Little Pigs now concur on this point,
Not wanting their wolf foe to topple the joint.)
The bankers insist that a low-interest loan
Is the safest foundation for any good home.

In a farm-kitchen photograph in *Elle Decor*,
"Home" means seagrass on a white-oak floor.
Kilims on concrete are actually best,
Counters a columnist writing for *Nest*.

Benjamin Moore and Farrow and Ball
Firmly maintain that paint color is all:
Home is Swiss Coffee or Williamsburg Stone,
Wevet, Gray Owl, Dead Salmon or Bone.

Waving away all this decorative stuff,
Sentimentalists claim that the home's in the heart:
In the memories you have of your mom and your dad.
True, the shrinks answer, but this can be bad—
Home is the place where your problems all start,
Where you'd do best to leave when the going gets tough.

In high school English—just ask any teacher—
Homecoming dramas reliably feature.
To get home, Odysseus braved epic odds
And spent a whole decade defying the gods.
Huck Finn ran away to escape a cruel Pa,
Then found a new home after breaking the law.
These books might be gathering dust on your shelf,
But their stories of home are songs of the self,
Of characters molded, discoveries made
(Or so say the notes that I took in tenth grade.)

Isn't home where you hang your proverbial hat?
No, crows the family, home is We.
No, cries the singleton, home is Me.
Yet home is a smell to a dog or a cat.
To a gardener, home is a favorite tree;
To a dreamer, a chair with a view of the sea;
To a lover, a key waiting under the mat.

Others say, home is our fate;
Others say, home is our state.
Others say, talking proudly
And rather loudly,
Home keeps *them* out,
Or else our greatness is in doubt.
Others speaking more softly say,
More and more
With each passing day,
Home is no more;
Home has gone away.

If today's many crises have troubled the notions
That used to inform our discussions of home;
If parents and children are faced with evictions,
If more and more people are dying alone,
And I no more than you,
Know what we should or should not do—
Though we know we cannot condone
The needless suffering of countless men,
And of countless women too—
Then I can't say "Home is" again.

All I can do is offer you,
Timidly,
A timid simile,
Borrowed from a poet far better than I:
Like love, I say.

Like love, we don't know where or why;
Like love we can't compel or buy;
Like love we often weep.
Like love we seldom keep.

DECO VASE OF ROSES (EDITH WHARTON), 2020
GOUACHE ON ARCHES PAPER

CLARE POTTER

THE PIECES THAT I MAKE are not meant to take the place of natural flowers or fruits and vegetables, but rather meant to give a sense of joy in something else—something special and amusing, unique and handmade that can add to a person's home. My garden and my home have always been intertwined with my work, and although most of my ceramic pieces go to others, I try to keep a few in my home that have special meaning to me.

Two silver baskets full of an assortment of my ceramic fruits and flowers rest on library bookshelves and a ceramic bowl of spring peas and their flowers has found a place on a side table. But the piece that has particular meaning to me is a basket of gardenias that sits on a table in front of a couch in my living room. It reminds me of happy times and gives me a sense of pride and comfort whenever I enter the room and see it.

In this difficult time that we are all in, that "special something else" has more meaning than ever and our appreciation of home is stronger than ever before.

CHARLOTTE MOSS: You're half American and half British and have lived all over the world. Where is home for you?

CLARISSA WARD: I used to say that home could be anywhere with AC and a working internet connection. Now that I have a family, home is London.

CM: You have covered the Syrian and Rohingya refugee crises closely. What's the impact on people of being forced from their homes?

CW: It's easy to forget, but very few people choose to leave their homes. Home is family, friends, familiar places, and smells that carry meaning and memories. To be forced to leave one's home is deeply traumatic.

CM: Where's the most unusual place you've had to spend the night?

CW: The airstrip of the Baghdad airport was certainly unusual (and uncomfortable).

CM: What are you afraid of?

CW: Anyone in my team getting hurt, anyone I love getting sick. Also, rats.

CM: What would you tell a young journalist starting out their career today?

CW: Buckle up, it's going to be a bumpy ride.

CM: What, if anything, shocks you?

CW: Cruelty. I have seen so much of it, yet I still find it so hard to understand.

CM: What is your favorite journey?

CW: A long walk in the beautiful Provençal countryside around my parents' house.

CM: What is the sweet spot of your day?

CW: Crawling into bed at the end of a long day and watching a great documentary or drama.

CM: Is there anything about you that people might be shocked to know, or perhaps just find illuminating?

CW: I have an American accent and a British accent, and I can move between the two easily, depending on who I am talking to. It's like being bilingual but utterly useless.

CM: Who is your favorite hero of fiction?

CW: I have always loved Anna Karenina, since I first read the novel at fourteen. She is not a classical heroine. In fact, she's deeply flawed but the best characters often are!

CM: What book is on your bedside table?

CW: *The Precariat* by Guy Standing, *Blood and Oil* by Bradley Hope, *Slavery and Islam* by Jonathan A. C. Brown, *Putin's People* by Catherine Belton.

CM: What's your personal style signifier?

CW: I almost always wear my hair up.

CM: What's your go-to wardrobe, your outfit *du jour.*

CW: In the field, it's usually a good pair of jeans with a loose but well-cut button-down shirt and probably a scarf for color or to cover my hair if necessary.

CM: What is your greatest extravagance?

CW: Nannies. I couldn't do my job and travel the way I do without great support.

CM: When I'm not working, I'm . . .

CW: Spending time with my sons and plotting what I want to work on next.

CM: Is there something you still want to learn?

CW: Farsi.

CM: What do you most value in your friends?

CW: Laughter and loyalty.

CM: Who are your heroes in real life?

CW: Doctors and nurses and firemen. Rescue workers.

CM: Which talent would you most like to have?

CW: I would love to play a musical instrument well.

CM: When you are traveling, what "visual" of home is always top of mind?

CW: Eating breakfast around the kitchen table with all my boys.

CM: Next travel destination for pleasure?

CW: Oman.

CM: Guilty pleasures?

CW: I am ashamed to admit that when I am on a tough assignment in a chaotic place, an occasional cigarette is still one of life's great pleasures.

CLARISSA WARD

October 2016, Northern Iraq

CLAUDIA WEILL

During the pandemic as our lives shut down, I found myself looking inward.
Home became the image in the mirror.

MICHAEL BOODRO

The Habit of Home

THE PROBLEM—and the charm—of home is that it is as much a feeling as a place. How often do we tell our guests to make themselves at home? In our offices—when we had offices—we prompted our visitors to feel at home.

What exactly provokes a feeling of home? Is it a sense of belonging, of safety, of relaxation and ease? Why do we feel at home in some places and not others (including in some people's homes)?

Those of us in the design industry would love to believe that it is an aura of beauty, a well-designed and well-functioning place, that transforms a house into a place we love. We want to believe that beautiful furniture counts, that hand-painted wallpaper, a custom rug, sumptuous fabrics, or curtains with passementerie trims are what makes us appreciate and love our homes.

But I am not so sure.

When I was a kid, my family moved often, which is perhaps why, as an adult, I have been so loath to change residences. I tend to hold on to my homes—with all their pleasures, faults, and discontents. But recently, after more than twenty-five years, for a number of reasons, we finally sold our weekend home in upstate New York and bought another, smaller retreat closer to the city. This was not an easy decision, and it tormented me for months. I couldn't imagine such a big change.

What would I miss, what would I remember, what would I mourn?

Home etches a map in your brain that has to do not so much with landmarks as movement. It is the paths and patterns of our days, the stair that always creaks when you head down each morning to make coffee, the water pressure in the shower and the low murmur of the dishwasher after dinner, the worn velvet on the arm of a club chair, even the zipper in a cushion cover that manages to irritate even as you are taking a nap. It is your ability to deftly and unthinkingly maneuver around the sharp corner of the coffee table. It is knowing precisely where to reach in the freezer to grab ice for a drink.

Home is a process. It is the way we move through the day. It is a starting point and a destination, a place of refuge, and a haven where we recharge. Most importantly, it is the people we share it with, the people we invite in, and the memories of all that we celebrate and grieve there.

Home is a habit, and familiarity breeds contentment. Until it doesn't. The eye gets tired, fashion changes, the fabrics get frayed, and reality—in the form of births and deaths, marriages and divorces, promotions and relocations—intrudes. That is what keeps the design business in business.

What was most surprising about leaving our weekend house was how easy the transition proved to be, how moving out of a home that I had labored over, improved, customized, and loved turned out to be almost effortless and virtually free of emotional drama. Yes, I miss the landscape of open fields and rolling hills, my roses and hydrangeas, and sitting on the porch, watching fireflies on a summer night. I miss the ways shafts of sunlight struck the rust walls of the living room, and the perfectly shaped maple tree in the front yard.

But now we have a new home.

Clients often become disconcerted when a new chair or table arrives, or a fresh paint color is put on the wall, and inevitably seems to dominate a room. The wise designer provides reassurance that within a week or so, the item will "settle in," become part of the larger, harmonious picture. In the exact same way, we need to "settle in" to our homes.

We have done that in our new place. We have crafted new paths, new patterns, and new memories. We have established new habits. We are once again at home.

CLINTON SMITH

*A*MIDST THE LIGHTNING-SPEED PACE at which new things are being launched into the world, it's easy to feel overwhelmed at times. Whether it's the latest tech gadget, a breakthrough in healthcare, or the newest social media platform, keeping up is both a blessing and a curse.

That said, the remarkable advances made in all aspects of our lives have reinforced my belief that the simple pleasures of home are more important than ever. A room you love has the power to comfort you, put you at ease and, perhaps, shield you from the demands and onslaught of stimulation coming from just beyond the threshold. I am not advising to retreat from it all, but a little reprieve never hurt anyone. The start of each day is always a great time to refresh, renew, and reflect a bit.

There is also something about creating an interior environment that fosters and forges lasting bonds, with both old friends and new acquaintances. Home should encourage both conversation and quiet thought. When the setting allows guests to move beyond small talk and chitchat and into topics that ignite passion points and activate communal thought, great things can occur. A world of possibilities, both big and small, awaits.

Sure, your home is also your escape, but it can also be a salon for ideation. A safe place where friends long to gather again to encourage each other. Perhaps it's gathering for dinner in a dimly lit room or enjoying a cocktail around the fireplace; perhaps a book club, or even a gossipy tête-à-tête. The sharing of new ideas, inspirations, challenges faced, and hardships won builds enduring and lasting relationships in a culture where so many things are ephemeral.

To be able to foster such an environment is a subtle gift, one learned through experience and study. A home doesn't have to be perfect, but like good manners, a gracious welcome never goes out of style.

CRAIG DYKERS

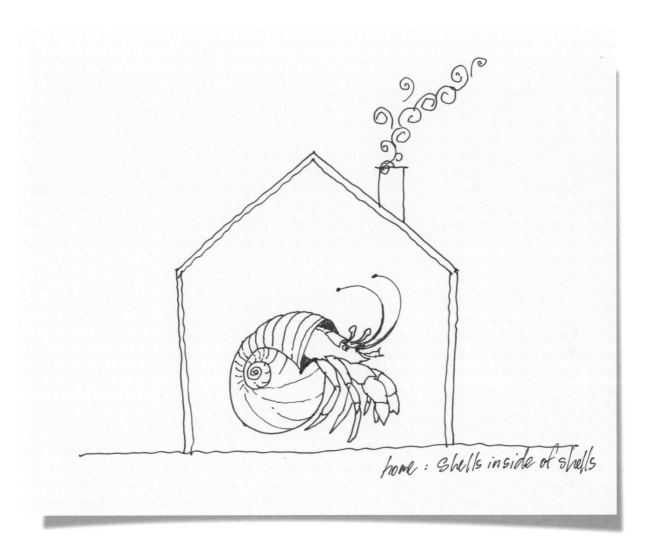

home : shells inside of shells

We inhabit a habitat of our own creation. Layers of shells upon shells. One shell is the home, a creature of protection and comfort. When should our homes challenge us? A home should not turn satisfaction into mere convenience to preserve the cocoon. Our home is also an invitation to explore worlds beyond.

DEBRA SHRIVER

Y FAVORITE NOOK IN OUR HOUSE is the small bricked-in courtyard. It is bordered by a series of French doors on one side, and a high, hand-cut brick wall on the other. Here, I indulge in what is perhaps my recurring Proust "madeleine" moment: just sitting and inhaling the fragrance of my late grandmother's petite gardenias. My Aunt Ruth brought them from her Florida garden with their roots floating in tiny jars of water, having already uprooted them once from their Alabama birthplace, her own mother's garden, stem by stem. These transplanted gardenias are to me the fanciest and the whitest of flowers, and give off the sweet long-ago scent of my grandmother's perfume. She adored gardenias, both in her garden and her toilette. The flowers bloom like miniature boutonnieres atop the leafy foliage. On late spring mornings, I often sit near them, as if in my own little world as I read the day's newspapers, still in my nightgown. The cold brick floor, beaded from the morning dew, cools my bare feet. I breathe slowly, and listen, not to the quiet, but to my own choir of noises: the cooing sighs of mourning doves who perch like statuary on the tops of my courtyard wall. They are joined by a cacophony of crickets, steamboat whistles, children playing in the Catholic school playground across the street, cathedral bells, the clop of horse hooves from the passing sightseeing carriages, and a duo of voices, one male and the other female. For every day, the "Pie Lady" sings out the fresh flavors of her homemade fruit pies a cappella as she pushes her small pie buggy through the streets of the French Quarter. "Mr. Okra" cruises slowly about the neighborhood in his farmer's truck, reciting in his bass-like, sing-song melody: "I have ok-ra . . . I have to-ma-toes . . . I have wa-ter-me-lon." As if performing a spontaneous duet, their voices rise above both sidewalk and street, and mingle midair into one sweet, tuneful aria.

All these sounds are comforting to me as I sit in my tiny, inner courtyard divided by half shade and half sun. There I have planted a mix of sago palms accented by my grandmother's white gardenias, and an occasional pink bromeliad. Each time we leave town for any period of time, the untended garden turns into jungle. The palmetto leaves grow so big that the sun's rising and setting projects large shadows on the side of the house. The leaves are heavy, and dance and wave in wind and rain, yet they always survive any storm or squall that passes over our home, much like New Orleans herself.

The palm fronds of our jumbo-sized banana trees hang low, the umbrella effect heightened by the sheer weight of the ripe, budding clusters. They bounce and wink at their faux image just beyond the French doors inside the kitchen. Beyond the landing, the Martinique banana-tree wallpaper made famous by the Beverly Hills Hotel offsets peach-colored terra-cotta floors.

Now that we have settled in, the house on Dumaine Street is like a character in our lives. After years of living in small urban spaces, we finally have a real house, big enough to gather all our friends. The dining room table, a much-beloved antique, is sturdy enough to hold a suckling pig. The house never disappoints,

and always upholds its end of the bargain. It welcomes and expands to meet the hordes of family and friends who come together on holidays and found weekends, and sometimes made-up occasions.

The house continues to pull us in, and soothe us. Once inside, we are rewarded by peace and quiet, which is, to me, one thing that no amount of planning, charm, money, or work can get you when you're in New York City. This is no longer the "faraway place" we travel to; it has become the "familiar." Here, inside its cool walls and brick-bordered courtyard garden, the house anchors my husband and me, but it also surprises us.

One afternoon on my way out, during our first spring there, I forgot to close the French doors at the end of the front hall leading to our courtyard. It was late April and a rainstorm lingered overhead. I turned the key to enter and was overtaken by the mixture of light and scent permeating the hallway from the garden. As twilight faded and night descended, a lone gas lantern flickered in the dusk, amid shadows of swaying banana leaves. Traces of wet soil and damp, moss-covered brick mingled with gardenia and sweet olive to fill the downstairs rooms. It was as though I had entered into my own secret garden. I stepped inside and closed the door behind me. I was home.

DAN BARBER

*I*STARTED COMING to Blue Hill Farm before my own memory of it kicks in. It's in there like DNA—the fields, the cows, the afternoon light. Naming my restaurants after the farm wasn't just a tip of the hat: it was an acknowledgment of place, its significance, the hold it can have on our bones. The big red dairy barn, the view from the kitchen table, centers it all.

Ever since my family moved suddenly from New York City to Blue Hill Farm at the beginning of Covid, that view of the barn has replaced the concrete and brick buildings we stared at from the place we used to call home. The barn is now the first thing the kids see in the morning and the last thing they see at dinner, before the light fades. At first it was like some strange, eerie vacation scene. Now it's home.

My daughters, seven and four years old, wake up in time for milkings; they make sure to wear their jackets with big pockets so they can collect eggs from the chickens. They love their eggs poached, but sometimes I'll go with scrambled.

My dad's signature dish was scrambled eggs—my mom died when I was four and my dad did not cook. Except scrambled eggs. He prepared them most weekend mornings—with margarine, sometimes a little salt, cooked to the point of no return. Those eggs didn't taste good or bad. They tasted of home.

But then one morning my aunt Tobé prepared breakfast. I was twelve at the time, home sick with strep throat, my dad away on business. I'll never forget watching her make the eggs, whisked over a double boiler, finished with French butter and tons of herbs. They were so soft they slid down my throat. I couldn't believe how delicious they were.

To be fair, I owe my love of those eggs to my dad. Without his dried out, tasteless version, my aunt's eggs would never have made an impression.

Sometimes it takes something dramatic—a change in scenery, a revelatory taste—and in an instant daily life gets turned upside down. Just enough to make you see what you've been missing.

SCRAMBLED EGGS
Serves 2

- 4 eggs
- 3 tablespoons milk, optional
- 2 tablespoons butter, softened
- ¼ cup mixed chopped herbs, such as parsley, chives, and dill
- Kosher salt and freshly ground black pepper to taste

In a medium bowl, whisk the eggs (and milk, if using). Place a double boiler over low heat, add the eggs, and keep whisking. (If you don't have a double boiler, use a metal mixing bowl set over a pot of barely simmering water.) Whisk just until the eggs begin to coagulate. They should be very soft and runny—be bold, take them off the heat before they overcook. Stir in the butter, herbs, salt, and pepper.

Blue Hill Barn
Edith Barber, 7 years old

Blue Hill Barn
Frieda Barber, 4 years old

DONALD ROBERTSON

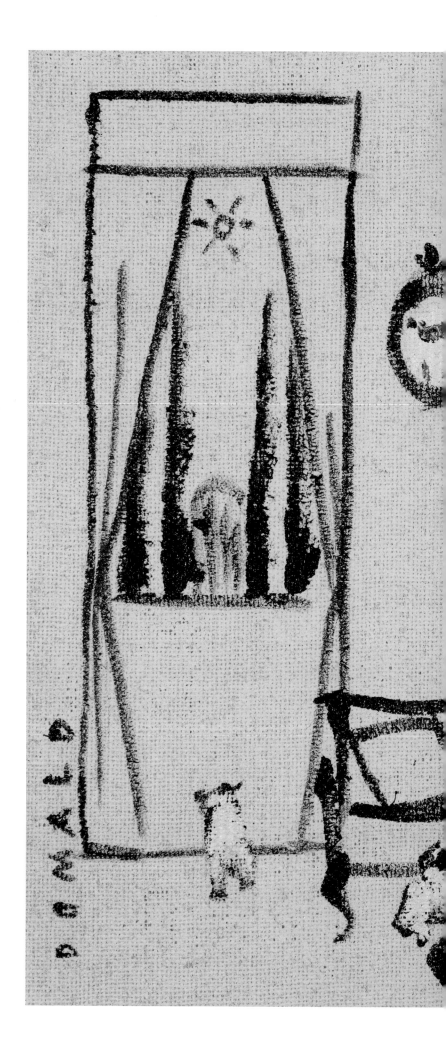

Home is where you hang your
dead or alive dog portraits.

At *home*

in THE *world*

Our understanding of home must extend beyond the four walls of our houses, the limits of our town, or even the borders of our countries. If recent times have taught us anything it's that we all share one home: the planet with all its beauty, diversity, and fragility. To travel is to enliven our sense of curiosity, but perhaps more than that it affords the opportunity to connect with people and place and it is in that connection we find comfort and ease with each other, respect that our fate is shared and we can feel, and indeed become, "at home in the world."

DREW BARRYMORE

I want to be cozy. I want things on my wall that are gathered
and curated. I like to have life on display. And then I
can feel the warmth of the decoration. I'm a collector—
I don't know how to live with a bare wall!

DEBRA MARTIN CHASE

*R*IGHT NOW, there is a banner on the facade of the New York Society for Ethical Culture that declares "Everyone deserves a place called Home." As the number of people who are homeless and residentially insecure increases exponentially during the global pandemic and as I daily see faces of despair on human beings who are tragically forced to live on the street, I have been moved to examine the importance of a place called Home in my own life.

My parents divorced when I was twelve and I was divorced by the time I was thirty. Growing up, there was often tension in the air in a house where the adults were loving, supportive parents but had outgrown each other long ago. There were a number of moves and different residences during my childhood and adolescence as my parents pursued first together, and later individually, career and life opportunities. Not unusually, during college and law school I lived in a different dorm or apartment every year.

When I married, I moved to a new city. As young, successful, and aspirational professionals, my then-husband and I moved several times until we both realized that fancier homes were not going to solve the problems within them. Single once again, I spent the next few years focused on building my career and my social life, which necessitated more moves and more residences. And so my peripatetic residential pattern continued until my spirit finally insisted that it was time to ground my soul and find my own place called Home.

Almost exactly twenty-four years ago, I entered a 1925 Spanish bungalow in the Hollywood Hills with a captivatingly expansive view of the city below and thought I just might have found my Home. The deal was sealed when I met the young son of the owners. He was one of the happiest kids I had ever met—bubbling with laughter and joy. I knew that if his spirit could thrive in that house, mine would too. I became the fourth owner of the dwelling that my family and friends refer to lovingly as Casa Chase.

As I settled in, the house began to tell me its story. The first owner was a silent screen actress turned successful businesswoman who owned the house for fifty years. I discovered a box of photos and mementos from her careers left behind in the garage. The next owner was a prominent motion picture costume designer. She lived there for the next twenty-five years. When I repainted the master bedroom, I discovered she had used the room as her studio and that the walls were completely covered with her imaginative designs. I know that the spirits of these artistic and independent women—and that of the joyous boy who only lived there a couple of years—infused the house with vibrant energy that continues to feed me to this day.

Casa Chase is my first real Home and we have a wonderful relationship. She has provided me with a peaceful retreat whenever I have needed to replenish my soul. She bolsters my power when I need to move at full speed. She has protected me when I was sick and supported me financially. I have been away for long periods of time and I have other residences, but she will always remain my Home and she always welcomes me back with open arms.

Perhaps because I did not really understand the need for establishing a place called Home until later in life, I do not take it for granted. I know that in order to be happy, healthy, and productive, people need a safe and secure place to live. While I will never come close to understanding the emotional and physical vulnerability of being homeless, I do know that feeling safe and secure should be a right, not a privilege, in one of the richest nations in the world. We must come together to find solutions for this problem. For hopefully we have learned collective lessons from the pandemic of 2020 and from being shut in for most of this year—that we are all part of a national community, that ultimately the problems of a few can and will affect us all, and that everyone does indeed deserve and need to have a place called Home.

HOME IS WHERE, 2020
INK ON ARCHES PAPER

THE RETURN (KEHINDE & TAIWO), 2020
COLLAGE (COTTON, SILK, BROCADE FABRICS, PHOTOGRAPHIC PRINT)

DURO OLOWU

A Bowl of New and Strange Fruit

IN A PALE BLUE ROOM with a white ceiling and matching cornices, their eyes opened to all that was new. Flicking from left to right as they encountered a flash of indigo, a stream of yellow, the lingering power of green. Colors were not yet a familiar sight but their senses were at ease. Caressed in folds of draped and tucked lace, cotton, and silk, they felt at home in this new world of human voices and whispers, fresh air and warmth. One voice seemed more predominant than others, that of the woman in whose arms they lay firmly but tenderly.

What was that thing above? Its blades spinning with the force of a hurricane. What was that distinct smell? A mélange of lemongrass and black soap awaiting their soft skin. What were the structures that filled the room? Furniture the size of buildings to newborn, untrained eyes. They waited for some kind of new disruption to a welcoming entrance into the world, unaware of the dangers averted that made it possible. And in that time, more colors flashed before them. Majestic brown, vivid orange, and African violet. Sometimes marked with subtle motifs of historical knowledge and power. Mixed, matched, and juxtaposed in a rousing cacophony of tones and crisply ironed and starched textures.

Suddenly they were both lifted from their mother's arms onto a scale. A murmur of approval was heard. The voices of two other women in the room were interrupted by a quiet tap on the door. A man entered with a beaming yet anxious smile, his teeth gleaming with delight as he walked toward the bed. He clasped his hands in gratitude and joy for the new additions to his life as he approached the mother and newborn children. Unsure of who to first caress, he began to weep until he took both from her and cradled them in his arms. Tiny, soft with glaring eyes and identical whiffs of black hair, they seemed comforted by the rocking motions he made.

What was he to do to protect them from the world and each other for as long as he could? How would he and their mother challenge and inspire their curious and mischievous minds in the early years so that they stayed innocent and unhurt for as long as possible? In this moment, he realized both the joy and burden of the wonders bestowed on them but hoped for the best.

BETTE MIDLER

BEFORE AND AFTER
Highbridge Park, Washington Heights

HEN I BEGAN my organization, New York Restoration Project (NYRP), back in 1995, I had no thought in mind but to right what I perceived to be a great wrong.

First, let me say how much I love nature. I love parks and gardens, and any outdoor space where I can refresh and renew myself, take in the changing of the seasons, and feel myself part of this beautiful planet.

I'm crazy about trees, flowers, fountains, ballparks, kids, and I think most people who live in New York love them too. The problem with New York, when I finally returned to it, after nearly twenty years in Los Angeles, is that many New York neighborhoods had no access to any of the things I just mentioned, and if they did, often those parks had been neglected or even abandoned for years, the fountains were broken, the walkways were strewn with garbage, and parents wouldn't let their kids into many of them because they simply were not safe. Many of them were used as chop shops; car thieves from all over the tristate area would drive stolen cars into parks, break them up for parts, and then set the carcasses on fire. It was just tragic.

To me, this was clearly an injustice, and not just to the people who had no access to open space that many take for granted, but an injustice to the land itself, which has no voice, and to the city as well, as a living, breathing organism.

In 1999, the department of housing, preservation, and development in New York had thousands of vacant lots on their books, and many opportunistic gardeners had been gardening on them for years.

BEFORE AND AFTER
Sherman Creek Park, Inwood

The city was getting ready to auction off 110 lots to developers for housing, but the gardeners who had been on those lots for decades protested by marching on city hall dressed as ladybugs and bees. They roosted in the trees across from city hall. It was a gigantic PR embarrassment for Rudy Giuliani, who was mayor at the time.

I, too, saw an opportunity. I just think that's how gardeners are. I contacted The Trust for Public Land, and together we raised enough money to buy the lots from the city at the price the city was asking. The rest is history.

These gardens have changed a lot of lives in New York. In these gardens, food is grown, birthdays and holidays are celebrated, children are taught environmental science, yoga classes happen, and movies are shown outdoors, raising everyone's spirits and letting the block know that they too are worthy of clean, green open space—which offers a sort of outdoor home to everyone.

So there you have it. The most rewarding work of my life was begun by picking up garbage in a public park. With this simple act, I demonstrated to New York that clean, green open space is a right, not a privilege.

Because of NYRP, I have seen parts of the city I never would have otherwise, met people I never would have met, learned to navigate city hall, and raised awareness among New Yorkers that nature is all around them, waiting to fall in love.

Here are some before and after photos . . . you can see why I am so proud of all New York Restoration Project has accomplished in twenty-five years.

ALEXANDRA PENNEY

When I returned to art after a detour in
journalism, I began by photographing peonies
and orchids. The painter Kenneth Noland
saw them and advised me to "keep working,
do a hundred a week, don't sleep. Make
flowers your own." More or less, that is what
I have done. Tens of thousands of pictures
later, flowers continue to give me pleasure.
Double pleasure, really, because the real things
always fill my apartment, lifting my spirits.

DANNY MEYER *and* LENA CIARDULLO

ARTWORK BY MAIRA KALMAN

ᴇᴀᴄʜ ᴅᴀʏ, before the lunch and dinner services, the staff at Union Square Hospitality Group's restaurants sit down to a "family meal." It is simple, often improvised, but some of the best food you'll never eat in a restaurant.

During these difficult times, these "family meals" have taken on a new meaning to our restaurant families. Besides being a celebration of food, they are a celebration of the restaurant's often-unsung heroes. This is home for the culinary community.

—ᴅᴀɴɴʏ ᴍᴇʏᴇʀ, *chief executive officer of Union Square Hospitality Group*
and member of Share Our Strength board of directors

As a child, I hated beans. I remember my mom making a fourteen-bean soup; I believed that this "dirty sludge" was a special kind of torture made just for me. I avoided them for much of my adulthood. When I first tasted this version (recipe opposite), my opinion completely changed. Beans are delicious and healthy, and can pack a ton of punch in the flavor department when cooked in this style. Nowadays, I love to make a big batch of beans and use them for all kinds of dishes, especially one of my favorite winter comfort foods, Pasta e Fagioli, which I make as a pasta dish tossed with herbaceous creamy beans and lots of olive oil.

—ʟᴇɴᴀ ᴄɪᴀʀᴅᴜʟʟᴏ, *executive chef at Union Square Cafe*

HEIRLOOM BEANS WITH GARLIC AND HERBS
Yields 12 cups

- 1 pound dried heirloom beans, such as cranberry, northern white, or calypso
- Kosher salt (preferably Diamond Crystal)
- 1 cup extra-virgin olive oil
- 15 cloves garlic, peeled and smashed
- 5 sprigs rosemary
- 5 sprigs thyme

Soak the beans overnight. To soak, place the beans in a large bowl, add cold water to cover by 2 inches, and set in the refrigerator. The next day, the beans should be more tender to the touch and slightly plumped. Drain the water.

Put the beans in a large pot and add cold water to cover by about ½ inch. Set over high heat. When the water comes to a vigorous simmer, foam will rise to the top of the pot. Using a slotted spoon, skim the foam and impurities off the top of the pot and turn the heat down to medium-low.

Continue to cook the beans, stirring occasionally, until they are fully tender with a creamy texture. This can take anywhere from 45 minutes to 1½ hours, depending on the bean type.

When the beans are done, season with salt until the cooking liquid tastes like a well-seasoned broth.

In a small sauté pan set over medium heat, add the olive oil and the smashed garlic cloves. Cook until the garlic is tender and turns golden-brown.

Turn the heat up to high and add the rosemary and thyme; the herbs will frizzle. When they stop bubbling, turn off the heat and pour the entire contents of the sauté pan into the pot of beans.

Let the beans steep with the garlic-herb oil. Before serving, remove any whole sprigs of thyme and rosemary.

PASTA E FAGIOLI
Serves 4 to 6

- Kosher salt
- 1 pound dried pasta, such as fusilli giganti
- 4 tablespoons extra-virgin olive oil, plus more for serving
- 3 cloves garlic, thinly sliced
- 1 sprig rosemary leaves, chopped
- 1 teaspoon red pepper flakes
- 2 cups Heirloom Beans with Garlic and Herbs, plus their cooking liquid
- ¼ cup chopped parsley
- ½ cup grated Pecorino Romano cheese, plus more for serving

In a large pot of boiling, well-salted water, cook the pasta just to al dente. Reserve 1 cup of the pasta-cooking water before draining.

While the pasta cooks, heat a large sauté pan over medium heat, warm 3 tablespoons of the olive oil and toast the garlic. When the garlic is golden, add the rosemary and chili flakes to toast lightly.

Add the beans and bean-cooking liquid to the pan and stir. Add the cooked pasta with the reserved pasta water and cook to meld the flavors, about 1 minute.

Fold in the chopped parsley and the remaining 1 tablespoon olive oil.

Add the ½ cup Pecorino and stir to bring the sauce together. Serve immediately with additional cheese and olive oil.

DOUG MEYER

*G*ROWING UP, I was always fascinated with tablescapes and still lifes. I would spend hours in my room *attempting* to arrange collections of objects and items that I collected. Inevitably, during or after my what-seemed-to-be daily attempts at tablescaping, my mother would come into my room, see what I had done and magically—within moments— perform a sleight of hand of rearranging things and voilà! It would be kind of perfect. I was always amazed while watching; it was so innate to her. I would afterwards study *why* it was so good—and began a new way of seeing compositions. I have always taken the knowledge that I learned from my mother and applied it to a lifetime obsession with arranging objects. Doing this always reminds me of growing up and home. And as such I practice my tablescaping skills all the time, especially when I travel. I take the objects I have (wallet, keys, plane ticket, receipts, pens, books, whatever) and create a still life—it is a way of always feeling a sense of home and sharing an experience I loved having with my mother. In this piece that I created for the *Home* book I wanted to do an obvious still life—but I wanted it to emphasize what I like in creating tablescapes. I like mixing disparate objects to create oddities and strange settings. I like to make the viewer stop and really stare at the arrangement. I don't like to create a classically beautiful setting, but one that has odd tension; in this case, none of the objects overlap. It's a strange blend of floral arrangements mixed with a child's alphabet blocks and stacked rocks that create a sculpture. All set in a somewhat sterile nondescript space.

STILL LIFE WITH BIRD, 2020
WOOD, PLASTER, EPOXY, PAINT, POWDER PIGMENTS, PENCIL, RESIN

ELEANORA KENNEDY

SO MANY BEAUTIFUL HOUSES ... an iconic beach house perched on a sand dune along the ocean's shore in Wainscott. A historic art deco apartment overlooking the jewel that is Central Park, a stone cottage in Ireland, and a quaint Key West cottage in West Palm Beach. How blessed I was to have shared these homes with my beloved husband, Michael. But now they are just houses; *he* was home. During our marriage, everywhere we'd spent any time together was transformed into a home—safe, secure, fun, and loving. Now, without him, the houses have become ghosts of joy for me.

The most recent house I left was called Kilkare, where I spent glorious summer months. Deep in January I can close my eyes and summon up those glorious days of summer on Georgica Pond. With my best friends. Talking ideas, facts, and gossip. Our children playing, circling around us in the warm sand, visits from our husbands. All accompanied by food, drink, and loyal dogs. This is where our children were raised, friendships nurtured, and milestones celebrated. Kilkare's porch a center of life and optimism. The dining room a weekly delicious sit-down of intellectual palaver ... South Fork artists, writers, politicos ... and so much dancing. All was in harmony. These were the best times of our lives.

Oh, the Niagara of memories.

The anniversary rockers from which we watched the stars, or the sunset cocktails on the North porch. Michael's welcome at dinners, acknowledging each guest and their accomplishments. The killer margaritas and all the healing yoga in his Zen garden.

For years we talked about how wonderful life at Kilkare was, but confessed that, without one another, it would be meaningless. It was a house for two people in love, two people for whom love was everything. Over decades, we formed memories. Now, I am still remembering. My withering heights ... his wuthering blights.

The loss of home was swift, but not fast enough for me. After my husband's death, home was gone and I needed for Kilkare to follow. The decision to sell did not come lightly.

Once all meaningful possessions were packed, our beloved daughter and my rock, Anna, lowered the proud US flag that fluttered for years on a tall pole in the front yard. She buried it in her father's precious Zen garden, then we carefully packed his Buddha statues. On a blustery autumn day, moving vans slowly pulled away from Kilkare. I gazed once more at the desolate house, tears in my eyes . . . until I felt him. Michael came with me on my new journey.

Michael was a rebel and a rogue. A dreamer. Suspicious of authority, entrenched in justice, he possessed fierce courage, stunning eloquence, and compassion, always underscored with love. He was stronger and braver than anyone I have ever known. The first time he put his arms around me I knew that no one and nothing could ever harm me. And it was true.

Now I go to nature to be home with him. He comes back to me often as I amble in solitude through the woods that surround my new house on the Hudson River. Among the ancient trees—one in which a mighty eagle has built his nest—Michael's Buddhas now dot the land and fill me with life-healing energy. He comes back to me in whiffs of fragrant bushes and soft flowers. Orchids in West Palm Beach say his name. He comes back to me again and again and when he does, I am home. When I'm lost, distressed, confused, or anxious, he speaks to me and I become still inside.

He taught me to be brave and that love requires courage. When I question whether I have the strength to continue, Michael is there and says yes.

When I'm searching for words to speak truth to power, he is there.

When I wonder if I can love, he is there.

When I'm faced with a choice between acquiescence and struggle, he is there and says, "Choose the latter."

When I am outraged, I see Michael smiling at me. He understood outrage.

Michael was, will always be, my safe place, my biggest adventure. He left me his magic.

Senza fine.

Tree frogs constellate

the august night, toes
splayed like satellites'
landing gear on the pane
where a plugged-in sun
posts a night-long dusk.

Pinpoints of light—
spectral lacewings,
moth-winged shuttles,
meteoric beetles—
clutter the astral chart.

Several evenings, transfixed
by the frogs' shifting vigil,
I've glimpsed a wraith of me—
scouring a skillet from lunch
or grinding the morning beans—

a torso with full-moon nipples
that expands this eclipse
of space and species where
I witness how minute,
how infinite, I am,

and how much further home
must reach.

IRIS APFEL *and* HUTTON WILKINSON

HUTTON WILKINSON: Iris, we're so fascinated by your childhood meeting with Elsie de Wolfe. How did you come to know her?

IRIS APFEL: My father was kind of a renaissance man; he did many things—he had a business working with glass and mirror. He could do very special things with mirror that nobody else could do. There came a time when Conrad Hilton had a project at the Plaza Hotel in New York City—he was trying to bring celebrities to the Plaza and had dedicated one entire floor to having a number of apartments done with various types of people in mind. Elsie was called upon to do the decorating, and she got an apartment.

HW: That's right, and so did Cecil Beaton, and I think Oliver Messel, all kinds of great designers.

IA: Right. My dad did practically all of the mirror work on the whole floor, and Elsie wanted him to work for her, to do the mirrors in her apartment. He said he'd be very happy to take the job, but she stipulated that she wanted him personally to do it. And he said, "I'm so busy, I can't handle it during the week, but since you are who you are, I would be willing to do it on weekends." So they struck up a deal, and Daddy went for several weekends and every time he went, he came back raving. There was this one particular Saturday, he came back just in heaven. He said Elsie had gotten a shipment of all of these beautiful, beautiful, simple French antiques. And he knew I was interested in all that kind of stuff and that I would go gaga if I saw them—and would I like to see them? And I said, "Oh my God, anything,

I would just adore it." He said, "Okay, tomorrow I'll ask Elsie if she would be kind enough to let you come one Sunday." So sure enough, he came home and said she was very sweet and I was to come next weekend. So on the appointed day, I went. Daddy was already working. I rang the bell and was buzzed in to this very large bedroom. I was in my early teens and of course my eyes almost popped. She had Blu Blu, in her lap and he jumped down and he started to jump all over me. He was kissing me so I figured "Gee, I'm in!" He was a darling, small-scale poodle and, as his name implied, he was colored a deep shade of blue. He looked as if he had just been dipped into a bowl of indigo.

And Elsie would sit there like she was holding court. She'd never get out of bed. She would sit in bed and I was the audience. She regaled me with all kinds of wonderful stories. And I was so fascinated with her bed jacket that I paid a compliment. She thanked me and said that she had this old flannel job and needed a new one. She was then inspired to have it copied in fur. So she sent the jacket to Maximillian the leading furrier of the day. They couldn't quite decide which pelts worked best, so they ordered several. I remember there was broadtail, chinchilla, sable, and mink. Whether she was wearing sable or mink that first day, I couldn't say, I was too young at that time to know the difference. Whatever!

HW: And she had a Brooklyn accent. Didn't she speak with a Brooklyn accent?

IA: To tell you the truth, I was so enamored, she could have talked Chinese. It was beautiful.

HW: I love that. Well, she was a real influencer. She really got you going, probably got you thinking about a lot of things in a lot of different ways.

IA: Oh she certainly did.

HW: Now, tell me about your own house. You've probably have had many, many houses in your life.

IA: No, I haven't, strangely enough.

HW: What, really? Oh, that's nice.

IA: I lived at home until I was married. And then we had an apartment, a very unusual apartment on the Upper East Side, very close to Central Park. It was a divine home. What it had in charm it lacked in plumbing! Its interior was falling apart, but it was quite a beautiful old relic. It was crazy. Anyway, we lived there for twenty-seven years. We had fourteen-foot ceilings with beautiful Rococo plasterwork and boiserie in the hallways. It was really a wild place.

Fortunately, we had wood-burning fireplaces to help with the breezes that blew through the chinks in the great bay windows and made it feel as if we were living in a drafty château.

HW: Did you decorate it yourself?

IA: Oh, yes. I was in the decorating business.

HW: Oh, I see. I knew about your iconic textile business Old World Weavers of course. But I didn't know that you also did decorating, how wonderful.

IA: Oh yes I started by being in the decorating business; I had quite a nice little business going. I had some very nice clients, and some crazy ones.

HW: I bet you did. So, between your own homes and those you decorated for clients, what makes a house a home? What makes it yours?

IA: Well, to me, expressing yourself. I hate standard equipment. And unfortunately today's decorating is—well, the more expensive it is, the worse it gets. You walk in and you think you're in a very, very expensive, umpteen-thousand-dollar-a-night hotel suite.

PHOTOGRAPH BY KEITH MAJOR

HW: And you don't know what city you're in, because all those hotel suites—in New York, Bangkok, Paris—they all look the same.

IA: They all look alike. They have no personality. And so many people strive to have an apartment like that. I think everybody has a history. And I think you should have bits and pieces of where you were and what you did and what you bought. And I'd rather have an apartment that has some mistakes in it than something that is so damn perfect. I'm very much for personality and expressing yourself.

HW: Exactly, and memories too—you bought that on that trip, that was given to you by that friend. It's so wonderful to have those memories and things from your family.

IA: Then we sold the building we had lived in for almost three decades and I was looking desperately for a loft on Park Avenue, which of course I couldn't find. But what I found was even better—a delightful apartment on Park Avenue that I have lived in ever since. So that one, and the two apartments I've had in Palm Beach—those are all of the homes I've had, which for being almost a hundred years old isn't very many.

HW: You're rare. Elsie de Wolfe certainly used to move every year I think, certainly back in the 1800s. I've had lots of houses and I'm just, you know, starting out!

IA: No, no, no, I can't, I have so much stuff.

HW: Did you ever have a favorite or are they all your favorites?

IA: Well, they're all different. They're all me, but they're all different. My house in Palm Beach is much more playful. It's full of antiques, but it's full of stuffed animals and crazy things, too, mixed in with some period pieces. And my home on Park Avenue is much more serious. I don't have a set of anything, I don't have a set of dining room chairs. I have a small table with four different ones.

HW: Oh, I think that's great. I love that. What about entertaining? Do you like to entertain?

IA: My husband, Carl, and I entertained a lot. We liked small dinner parties at home. I always had a very good cook, and we always entertained that way. And then my husband was a very good—of all things—Chinese cook! So we used to have Sunday nights and—those were big, big events, you know, a lot more people and we loved it.

HW: Let's talk about individuality in the home and let's talk about your need for individuality, because apparently out there in the world, when we walk on the streets, there's a lot of people who don't want to be individual. They all want to wear t-shirts and blue jeans.

IA: Well, I feel that's just a terrible thing. I think they're wasting their lives because God did not make everybody in the same image and everybody is an individual. All these beautiful young girls don't know how to wear clothes. They have beautiful figures and they'll put something on and it looks like a rag because they don't know how to carry it. They all want to fit in. And I, myself, never set out to do any of these things to shock anybody or to change anything. I just do it because I like to do it. And I like to be happy with myself. I'm not like everybody else. So I can't dress like everybody else. And, therefore, I don't think like everybody else. People ask me all the time what my design philosophy is and I always tell them that to me, the same aesthetic rules and the same design principles apply, whether we're talking fashion or home decor. It's just that in one, I dress a body and in the other one, I dress a space.

HW: You know what you have, Iris, that other people don't have? You have a wonderful sense of fantasy. And I think a lot of these houses and a lot of these decorators just take it all too seriously.

IA: Oh, they're so serious. The world is so gray. We need color and fantasy. In my cradle, I received a few gifts. The wise men came, and they gave me a sense of humor and a sense of curiosity and a sense of fantasy. And they have stood me in good stead. I don't think I'd have gotten this far if I didn't have those.

HW: Now let me ask you, are there certain things that you feel every home should have? What are the most important elements of a home?

IA: You mean like a bed or indoor plumbing?!

HW: Ha! No, what makes a home homey to you?

IA: Being surrounded by things that I like.

I love, love animals, but I don't have real ones. So I have wonderful stuffed animals. I have all kinds of them. And I have a great passion for Mickey Mouse. I have a lot of small ones, and I wanted a great big one and my husband would never buy him for me; he said it was ridiculous. So on my ninetieth birthday, I happened to walk into Costco just as a big crate arrived, and I watched them open it. Out fell dozens of Mickey Mice—in a very, very big size!

HW: Oh, how wonderful.

IA: They were selling for the enormous price of $32. So I said to myself, "Oh my God, all my life I wanted one, nobody ever bought me one, and it's my birthday. I'm going to buy myself a Mickey Mouse." So I gifted myself a big one and I dragged him home. And I was so happy with him. And very shortly thereafter, I was invited to speak at the Tribeca Film Festival. And after the speeches and everything, we sat around talking and we got on the subject of Disney. And I confided how mad about Mickey Mouse I was, and how I love my big one. And two days later, my bell rang and this huge package was at my door and it was a second Mickey Mouse, the same big one. So I brought him to Palm Beach, where he fell in love with my big, painted baby grand player piano—it's really a mad thing. But I think it inspired him to try to be a concert pianist. He sits there all day practicing. I don't have the heart to tell him he stinks. I just let him bang away. Whatever!

EMILY EVANS EERDMANS

The Day We Took the Blue Bows Down...

ISMANTLING THE HOME of my friend and mentor Mario Buatta after his death was one of the most intense experiences of my life. I was by his side when he died, but I felt him deeply over the next year as I spent time organizing his most cherished possessions. His apartment—and all the glorious items in it—meant everything to him, and, as he himself admitted, in many ways took the place of a partner or companion.

Mario's living room, decorated in 1976, was one of the most influential rooms of the late twentieth century, and many people commented that it should be donated in its entirety to the Smithsonian. Instead, it was gradually disassembled and dispatched to various auction houses—all except for these three bows. For nearly forty-five years they stood proudly over Mario's prized collection of dog pictures that he always jokingly referred to as his family portraits.

Mario loved to say that a house is a scrapbook of one's life, and it was the case times a million for him. As I researched each piece and began to understand how his mind worked, I understood more deeply how each piece reflected his enthusiasms and his eye, and consequently I began to understand *him* more deeply. Mario often opined, "Pulling together a home is not something that can be accomplished overnight. I compare the process of designing to the way a painter approaches a canvas. It happens slowly—one dab at a time—until the overall effect is pleasing. And over a period of years, every room will tell a story—one that is unique to the people who live there."

The day Sotheby's started taking the dog pictures down, I was consumed with emotion at seeing the room come undone. As it dissolved, so did his presence—which is why we kept the bows, and in a way Mario, in place until the very last moment.

ABOVE: PHOTOGRAPH BY SCOTT FRANCES

ENUMA OKORO

A Worldly Home

GREW UP WITH A MOTHER who had a love for both travel and interior decorating. Our chairs and sofas were always being replaced or reupholstered. Bedroom sets would come in and out. Dining room consoles designed and delivered. And with every trip my mother took, she'd come back with suitcases of artifacts, and shipped boxes of furniture from a country my siblings and I had yet to visit. Our house, wherever it's been over the decades, Nigeria, America, Côte d'Ivoire, or Tunisia, always hinted of a larger world beyond its doors, just waiting to be explored. But as kids at home, we slid our socked feet on silk and wool rugs, and glided our little lithe bodies over brocade settees and thickly stitched tanned leather poufs. We dared each other to steal seconds on the forbidden seats of hand-carved Senufo stools, and when playfully scuffling about we edged our way around shelves heavy with porcelain vases from China and bronze statues from Burkina Faso. We were at home among these foreign things.

Sometime during third grade, while we were living in Nigeria, I started a curious pastime of spending afternoons designing my own future house in my head. Belly on my bedroom floor, legs kicked up and swinging behind me, lounging unladylike in some lovely little dress, I'd cup my hands in my chin and imagine the house I'd live in when I was grown up. Then later, at the dinner table or maybe in the car on the way to school, I'd tell my parents all about it, no doubt to prepare them for my inevitable move.

"I'm going to have a gigantic house, and I'll decorate each room to look like a different country," I'd say, beaming with pride at my eight-year-old plans. I remember clear as day, boasting as though it were all already a fait accompli, a mansion in some future land just waiting for me to age another twenty years. "I'll have the India room, the Egypt room, the China room, and the Greek room."

The most spectacular thing of it all was that I could imagine everything in each room, down to what the textured cushions and colorful rugs would look like, and what might hang on the walls. I thought my newfound passion was about design, which in some sense it was. In my little mind at the time, raised with the mother I had, interior design seemed the most logical passageway for my curiosity about what was beyond our doors. At some point along the way, I even declared to my siblings that I no longer wanted to be a pianist when I grew up. I wanted to be an interior decorator. But really, what my mother was passing down to me through her own habits and inclinations was a growing familiarity with difference, and an appreciation for diversity. Her love of interior decorating and travel nourished my own unique sensibilities to wander through and to wonder at the world. And the home she was constantly re-creating for us was a slow but consistent intimation for imagining ourselves as comfortable in the world as we were in our own home.

So this is how, from a very young age, I imagined my own future life, craving a particular kind of intimacy with the world. I understood it was full of a diversity of cultures, and I suppose I wanted to live within that diversity in ways that felt as close and secure as my own childhood home. I had already begun to desire waking up in spaces infused with the spirit I sensed of how I would eventually make my own way in the world, living and working across borders and countries. Over the past few decades, it is what my life has turned out to be. I became a writer and a global lecturer and speaker. I travel endlessly with my mind and my feet. Rather than my home hinting of a wider world, I have made myself at home in the real world, recognizing and appreciating the ways in which different countries provoke my imagination, and evoke different sides of me. Just like that imaginary house from my childhood musings, where I floated through rooms symbolic of different countries. Only now, the vision is embodied in even more transformative ways that include the beautiful exchange of life and love between a global diversity of people. It's a particular way of understanding my place in the world, never static, always shifting and slanting, allowing the varied nuances of "homeness" to slip over me once I step onto what always becomes familiar soil. Nigeria, Morocco, Côte d'Ivoire, Italy, France, America, England: these countries coax different energies out of me and remind me that I've got a few skins I'm quite comfortable in. I carry multiple homes within me.

DAYLE HADDON

Home is first a doorway that welcomes me back.

Home is where I return to replenish my being,
a nest where I can safely build my dreams, rest my
body, and just be, instead of do.

Home is a reflection of the inner me, lovingly
curated to speak to me of who I am today. I have
created a new world by my choices that tells
a story, holds a memory, captures a feeling, all an
affirmation of who I am now, and sings to me . . .
yes, yes, you are home!

Home is music to my soul as it resonates my
choices back to me.

Home is harmony, love, peace, rest, contemplation.

Home is my heart beating back to me.

Home is me.

I am home!

HOME, 2020
OIL ON CANVAS

GLORIA STEINEM

Coming Home

A S I WRITE THIS, I'm fifteen years older than my father was when he died.

Only after fifty did I begin to admit that I was suffering from my own form of imbalance. Though I felt sorry for myself for not having a home, I was always rescued by defiance and a love of freedom. Like my father, for instance, I'd convinced myself that I wasn't earning enough money as a freelancer to file income tax returns, something I had to spend months with an accountant to make up for. Like him, I'd saved no money, so there was a good reason for my fantasy of ending up as a bag lady. I handled it by saying to myself, *I'll organize the other bag ladies.*

Finally, I had to admit that I too was leading an out-of-balance life, even if it was different in degree from my father's. I needed to make a home for myself; otherwise the lack of one would do me in, too. Home is a symbol of the self. Caring for a home is caring for one's self.

Gradually, the rooms that I had used mostly as an office and a closet were filled with things that gave me pleasure when I opened the door. I had a kitchen that worked, a real desk to spread papers on, and a welcoming room where visiting friends could stay, something I'd always wanted as a child when I was living with my mother in places too sad to invite anyone. Though it was a little late, after fifty, I even began to save money.

After months of nesting—and shopping for such things as sheets and candles with a pleasure that bordered on orgasmic—an odd thing happened: I found myself enjoying travel even more. Now that being on the road was my choice, not my fate, I lost the melancholy feeling of *Everybody has a home but me*. I could leave—because I could return. I could return—because I knew adventure lay just beyond an open door. Instead of *either/or*, I discovered a whole world of *and*.

Long before all these divisions opened between home and the road, between a woman's place and a man's world, humans followed the crops, the seasons, traveling with their families, our companions, our animals, our tents. We built campfires and moved from place to place. This way of traveling is still in our cellular memory.

Living things have evolved as travelers. Even migrating birds know that nature doesn't demand a choice between nesting and flight. On journeys as long as twelve thousand miles, birds tuck their beaks under wings and rest on anything from ice floes to the decks of ships at sea. Then, once they arrive at their destination, they build a nest and select each twig with care.

I wish the road had spared my father long enough to show him the possibilities of *and* instead of *either/or*. If he'd been around when I finally created a home, I might have had something to teach him, as well as time to thank him for the lessons he taught me.

I wish my mother hadn't lived an even more polarized life of *either/or*. Like so many women before her—and so many even now—she never had a journey of her own. With all my heart, I wish she could have followed a path she loved.

I pause for a moment as I write these words. My hand, long-fingered like my father's, rests on my desk where I do work I love, in rooms that were my first home—and probably will be my last. I'm surrounded by images of friends and chosen objects that knew someone's touch before mine—and will know others after I am gone. I notice that my middle finger lifts and falls involuntarily, exactly as my father's did. I recognize in myself, as I did in him, a tap of restlessness. It's time to leave—there is so much out there to do and say and listen to.

I can go on the road—because I can come home. I come home—because I'm free to leave. Each way of being is more valued in the presence of the other. This balance between making camp and following the seasons is both very ancient and very new. We all need both.

My father did not have to trade dying alone for the joys of the road. My mother did not have to give up a journey of her own to have a home.

Neither do I. Neither do you.

DIMORESTUDIO

A house isn't just walls and tables, it is also things
like the tableware you choose and the
placement of a cushion in a certain position.
It is filled with a nostalgic atmosphere of
yesteryear, conveying the impression that time
stands still and is unable to penetrate or
change the space. The extra magic created by
present-day elements, such as contemporary
art and furniture pieces crafted using innovative
techniques, also aids in keeping the original
spirit of the rooms. Upon first glance, the juxtaposition of these objects may seem simple,
but in all reality, it is thoughtful and sophisticated.

—EMILIANO SALCI AND BRITT MORAN

A good armchair represents comfort and repose.

KINSEY MARABLE

In 1971, novelist Anthony Powell wrote *Books Do Furnish a Room*. And, indeed they do. My house is full of books—not just in the library, but everywhere. The one place where I pay special attention is the guest room. Visitors need downtime, and nothing is more relaxing than finding an array of good books in one's room. No hand-me-downs, no paperbacks, but rather a combination of books that you have chosen because you have read and enjoyed them. And remember, the more the better.

THE GUEST ROOM LIBRARY

Alexander Hamilton by Ron Chernow

An American in Paris by Janet Flanner

The Best of Beaton by Cecil Beaton

Between the Woods and the Water by Patrick Leigh Fermor

Billy Baldwin Remembers by Billy Baldwin

A Christmas Memory by Truman Capote

The Compleat Martini Cook Book by Baba Erlanger and Daren Pierce

Directions to Servants by Jonathan Swift

Down the Garden Path by Beverley Nichols

Great Houses of Italy: The Tuscan Villas by Harold Acton

Happy Times by Brendan Gill and Jerome Zerbe

The Innocents Abroad by Mark Twain

Jean Howard's Hollywood: A Photo Memoir by Jean Howard

Liar's Poker: Rising Through the Wreckage on Wall Street by Michael Lewis

Mapp and Lucia by E. F. Benson

A Moveable Feast by Ernest Hemingway

The New Yorker Stories by Ann Beattie

An Omelette and a Glass of Wine by Elizabeth David

On the Road by Jack Kerouac

The Paris Wife by Paula McLain

The Remains of the Day by Kazuo Ishiguro

When the Moon Was High: Memoirs of Peace and War, 1897–1942 by Ronald Tree

Winston and Clementine: The Personal Letters of the Churchills edited by Mary Soames

DELIA KENZA

I selected this photo because it was at the
beginning of the Covid shutdown, and
all I could think about was not being able to
travel, and then I remembered the power
of memories. So, I took daily Covid-cations,
as my friend called them, going down
memory lane in my photo gallery. I realized
I have many homes because home
is where I feel happy, safe, and loved.

RENÉE *and* JOHN GRISHAM

Oakwood Farm

E BOTH GREW UP in the suburbs, and not too many years into our marriage realized that we longed for older things. That, plus the absence of a sense of place, of ancestral land, of the family home where grandmother lived and everyone returned to for the holidays, drove us to leave the cookie-cutter houses we knew so well. We moved to Oxford, Mississippi, our college town and the place we were married, and built our dream home on seventy-five acres. Since the house was brand new, and the floors didn't even squeak or give, we filled it with old furniture and ancient rugs. We settled in and planned to be content there for a long time.

Life and success intervened and we soon found ourselves looking for a temporary place to hide. We poked around central Virginia, and an old house found us. It was the first one we looked at, out of many, and the last one too.

We moved to Oakwood in 1994 for a one-year sabbatical of sorts, with plans to hustle back home to Oxford where we belonged and where our families were. But Oakwood had other plans.

The farm dates back to the 1700s and has been home to many over the centuries. The house grew as families prospered and fell into disrepair when they did not. A cemetery near the main house bears witness to those who lived and died on the land.

The house, a rambling country home with hints of Second Empire architecture, needed an extensive renovation, not to mention a new roof, a modern kitchen, and bigger bathrooms. Its porches were wholly inadequate for the serious loafing we contemplated. One project led to another. As layers were peeled away we realized that the old house should be protected and only slightly altered. We became enamored with its original construction and strove to preserve it.

Oakwood seeped into our very being. It became our sanctuary. And with time we realized that we would not leave it. It became home to us and especially to our children, and we wanted them to have that small, special piece of the world that they would always call home.

We discovered horses and built sheds and barns. We painstakingly renovated the outbuildings. One was used as a schoolhouse for the plantation's families and we converted it to a guest house.

The dilapidated and sagging summer kitchen became a fine and productive writer's cottage.

Our children grew up at Oakwood and still return almost monthly. They have their rituals, their memories, and their bedrooms, though these have now been taken over by the grandchildren. The farm has evolved and become a place for celebrations. It has hosted fiftieth wedding anniversary parties for both sets of our parents, and fundraisers, Easter egg hunts, Halloween tales by the cemetery, flashlight tag, garden club luncheons and tours, engagement announcements, baby showers, cutthroat bocce tournaments, long hot summer days by the pool, redneck croquet, family reunions, and countless late dinners on the porches. Oakwood loves to dress for a soiree: two weddings, two baptisms, a Scottish fiddle concert, equine events, an intimate dinner with a former First Lady.

While Oakwood's gardens are pretty, they are far from off-limits and meant to be used by family and friends. The secret garden hosts grandchildren's picnics while the goldfish swim nearby. The ancient boxwoods are great hiding places for children with their flashlights. The farm loves a party and the air fairly crackles with excitement. The energy is electric when Oakwood is filled with friends. It is a place long on tradition but quite busy with the present.

In the past two years we have researched the history of our farm and realized that we should somehow pause to honor the enslaved people who built it. We feel a responsibility to acknowledge and recognize them. We recently found the remnants of Oakwood's slave cemetery. Our research is a journey filled with sadness for a tragic history, but also filled with the hope of a reconciliation.

Oakwood welcomes this painful dig into its past and is slowly revealing its history. We find and learn more about this land every month. When the archeology is finished, Oakwood will throw yet another party and try to make peace with its history.

We are not blessed with the foresight of knowing how long we will enjoy Oakwood, and we spend little time pondering the future. The present is challenging enough. It is home, and home to our family and its next generation.

May we all be good stewards of the land we love.

ROSE NOEL

𝒲HEN WE THINK OF HOME, we think of comfort food and the care and feeding of friends and family. Nothing spells comfort quite like Fettucine alla Bolognese. This sauce is one of the most beloved in the Italian lexicon of food for good reason. Our secret to this foundational sauce? We use heritage Berkshire pork, fresh herbs, and lots of love.

FETTUCINE ALLA BOLOGNESE
Serves 6 to 8

HOMEMADE PASTA (RECIPE FOLLOWS)

BOLOGNESE SAUCE

- Parmigiano-Reggiano or Pecorino Romano rind, optional
- 2 bay leaves
- 8 sprigs thyme
- 3 sprigs oregano
- 1 teaspoon red pepper flakes, ground
- 1 teaspoon fennel seeds, ground
- 1 teaspoon black peppercorns, ground
- Extra-virgin olive oil
- 1 cup carrots, finely diced
- 1 cup celery, finely diced
- 1 cup Spanish onion, finely diced
- 1 tablespoon tomato paste
- 1 cup dry red wine
- 3 cups pork or veal stock (chicken stock can also work)
- 5 pounds ground pork
- 5 pounds ground beef
- 2 (28-ounce) cans tomato sauce
- 2 cups heavy cream
- 1 cup finely grated Pecorino Romano cheese, plus more for serving
- Kosher salt to taste

Make a sachet: In a piece of cheesecloth, place the rind (if using), bay leaves, thyme, and oregano and tie closed with kitchen twine; set aside. In a spice grinder or mortar and pestle, grind the red pepper flakes, fennel seeds, and black peppercorns; set aside.

In a large pot set over medium-low heat, add a small amount of olive oil, just enough to cover the bottom of the pot. Add the carrots, celery, and onion and cook until tender, about 10 minutes.

Add the ground red pepper flakes, fennel seeds, and black peppercorns. Toast until aromatic, about 3 minutes. Add the tomato paste and allow it to cook and develop a brick-red color, about 5 minutes.

Deglaze with the red wine. When the wine cooks down, add the stock. Allow to reduce to about 25 percent of its original volume, about 7 minutes.

Add the ground pork and beef, tomato sauce, and the sachet. Cook for about 45 minutes, until meat is fully cooked, stirring occasionally. Add salt to taste.

Stir in the heavy cream and cook for 10 minutes more. Add the Pecorino Romano and stir to combine. To serve, top homemade fettucine with the sauce; serve extra grated cheese on the side.

HOMEMADE PASTA
Serves 6 to 8

- 4 cups "00" flour
- 1 cup semolina flour
- 1 tablespoon kosher salt
- 24 egg yolks (have an extra yolk ready, if needed)

Put the "00" flour, semolina, and salt into a stand mixer fitted with the dough hook. Add the egg yolks.

Mix on low speed for 6 minutes. The dough should just come together. Add in extra yolk if dough seems too dry.

Gather the dough into a ball and wrap in plastic wrap. At this point the dough should rest at room temperature for 30 minutes before sheeting and cutting or can be refrigerated for up to 24 hours.

DAVID G. BRADLEY

Unavailable on Multiple Listings

YOU WON'T FIND our tree house on multiple listings. It's really so much less than a house. The idea of spending the night in our tree house is best enjoyed at the idea stage and, depreciating by the hour, becomes intolerable by 5:30 a.m. when the sun comes out, the ants stream forth, and the children want to be carried (in their sleeping bags) into their "real" home.

Our tree house is less than a house. But it is very much a home. There's not a square foot of surface on that cheerful structure I can't remember watching my sons create. There are places, the tricky places, where I can remember the cut of a specific plank or the size of a screw eye. Maybe because we were so bad at making it, every place on the tree house is marked with a memory of me with my boys.

It is the marking with memories that draws us to our childhood homes or to the places we raised our own children. For some, it's their first apartment after college, or the newlywed home. But it's all mere structure, something less than a tree house, when no memories mark the place.

DEAN ASLEEP WITH HIS EYES OPEN

KITTY WIDE AWAKE

I would immediately say my dogs are the center of everything. I love being home with them more than anywhere. They inspire me. They make me laugh. They help me sleep. I love so much when Dean tries to appear awake, all the while I know he's fast asleep. And Kitty, wide awake, acting as sentry.

JAMIE BECK

The day I brought Eloise into this room,
home transformed from a physical space to
an emotional place. Home is not the box
in which we live, but the ones we belong to.
Eloise, my daughter, you are home to me.

JEFFREY DUNGAN

Home is a dream, it's a place I've never been, or even seen.

It's an echo of something invisible to the eye, but I feel it, still living deep inside my heart.

Home whispers to us in the spiritual way that music slips past our mind, speaking directly to our souls.

Home speaks in the emotional language of a piano, like a song sung by angels—of a place that could heal us.

Home is a promise, almost kept, that we still believe. Of the earth, on the earth—yet beyond it.

Searching and plying we find, only pieces and parts; passionately pursuing our dreams of home—

Always greater, ever elusive of our attempts to fully capture it.

JULIA REED

M Y HOUSE IN THE MISSISSIPPI DELTA was born on a legal pad in Birmingham's Highlands Bar & Grill over martinis with the gifted architect James Carter. That was in the winter of 2017, but its gestation had begun decades earlier. Almost ever since I'd left it for good, I'd been dreaming of a getaway in the place where I grew up, where so much and so many people that I hold dear still exist. Where I could let loose, ride a horse, throw a party on a sandbar, drive the levee at sunset, soak up the loamy chemical smell that is more powerful to me than any madeleine. There was my parents' house, of course, but much as I love them, sleeping in my brother's childhood twin bed was not what I'd been imagining. I needed a room, a house, albeit a small one, of my own. Toward the end of my marriage, the need became more urgent. I brought my friend Ellen to visit for the first time and she said she could feel my whole being exhale as soon as we crossed into the flatlands from the hills. When my mother announced she was selling our house, that did it—there was a sliver of land separated from our deep backyard by a tall wooden fence. It sat across a dirt road from the pasture where I once kept my horse and felt like it was much farther into the country than it actually was. *"Don't sell the land!"* I shrieked into the phone. She didn't, but she and pretty much everybody else told me I was crazy: there's no hookup for gas, water, or electricity; the resale value will be laughable; you don't really want to do this, you just think you do. As a child I was told—a lot—that I was hardheaded. Maybe, but even then I knew my own mind. In this case, my mind and my heart told me that this was exactly—finally—right.

PHOTOGRAPH BY PAUL COSTELLO

JILL KARGMAN

Home Is Where the Art Is

*I*N MY FAVORITE MOVIE, *Hannah and Her Sisters*, a rock star played by Daniel Stern is doing a studio visit, in search of a painting about three by five feet to go above his new sofa. Horrified, the artist snaps back, "I don't sell my work by the yard!" Throughout my life I've seen people shop under duress—scrambling to find a dress to wear to a wedding, the right shoes for that party, and I can honestly say I've never done that. I don't ever go out on a mission, and I've never asked for a friend's opinion as I weigh a purchase; I either love or hate things. I'm pretty black and white on just about everything: political opinions, taste, food, music, you name it.

Which is why it was so much fun to meet and marry a fellow art freak who loved going to fairs and seeing what's out there. My husband, Harry, and I always agree most of it is utter dreck and roll our eyes at the overpriced garbage floating around. But it's still fun to go look or gawk—to each his own, and difference is what makes the world go round (and the art market soar). Before we had our three children, we lived in a teeny one bedroom in a fourth floor walk-up. It barely had wall space for acquisitions and, even though we frequented many affordable art fairs in Williamsburg and visited artists' lofts in Bushwick, we couldn't really buy much we loved. But here and there we'd happen upon a graphic work on paper, or a photo collage that we'd buy and lean against the wall or a bookshelf. Through the years, and two more apartments, the framed pieces piled in front of each other and were cluttered against windows, leaning next to cribs, balanced on an overcrowded mantel.

Twenty years later, we are in our deathbed house that we will exit with toe-tags. When we moved in, we took all those cluttering frames and put them up on a big gallery wall. We gasped. Somehow, gathered from various places, from shitters to under our bed, all those lovingly gathered works Tetris'ed all together into a quirky mosaic of our life together. Each drawing a memory of age twenty-seven or thirty-two or forty-five, trips we took or a printmaker we met or a hovel gallery we happened upon. I look up at that wall and I see our marriage in art. I honestly don't give a shit about jewels or furs or whatever people get for anniversaries or birthdays. I prefer a quirky piece of art that fits into our very narrow style of calligraphic ribbons of black, lettering or currency, gothic darkness or dark thorny flowers, and of course skulls. I grew up with parents who loved Dutch *vanitas* paintings, always laden with food, pearls, and precious gems next to the skull, a reminder you can't take it with you. Make the most of the time you have and enjoy the fruit before it rots and the flowers before they fade.

While I've always appreciated each and every purchase, when Covid-19 hit and we were at home in New York City for four months straight without ever going outside for more than a few minutes a day, I feel like I found a renewed attachment to the wall. I spent so much time looking at each sketch or painting and being so overwhelmed with gratitude—for health and safety, for a roof over our heads, but also for a space filled with things we collected together.

I'll be honest: The word "collector" has always sounded so obnoxious to me. People are starving, so when I hear that word it sounds like pretentious bragging, like there are just bags of money lying around. But for us, so many of our purchases cost barely anything; one of my fave finds was a drawing from the

Clignancourt flea market for twenty euros. Some purchases have gone up in value considerably and some we couldn't get a hundred clams for. But it was never about buying stock in an artist; it was about things we love. While we are not hoarders and like a clean, uncluttered space, our living room wall is a map of our family's life. When I look at a Scott Campbell laser-cut made out of dollar bills, I also remember an anniversary. When I see Michael Bevilacqua's layered-vellum skeleton hand, I know it was a birth present when my son, Fletch, arrived. I see Tauba Auerbach's ink-on-paper letter *K* and know it's my maiden and married initial.

During the rush of normal life, art can seem like a mere backdrop to life. But during 2020 it was center stage. I would take time to stare at our pieces and appreciate every brushstroke or flick of a pen. I couldn't see my beloved bridesmaids or their kids but the wall felt somewhat like seeing old friends. Quarantine was clearly not a good thing, but if you're lucky enough to have a home you love coming home to, it was all the healing we needed during surreal, scary times. The art you choose for your home becomes almost a physical representation of your eye, the feelings it evokes in you are what you want to feel, and relishing them is a balm to the weary psyche of this moment. It provides a portal to happier times, when they came home with us into our young lives, and a pole-vault of hope for the future when it will be safe to drink in the creative, eclectic energy of art fairs once again.

PHOTOGRAPH BY STEPHEN KENT JOHNSON

JIM SHEPARD

Home and the Apocalypse

HEN MY MOTHER DIED six years ago, a family friend wrote to say that one of the things he loved about her was that she was never afraid to speak her mind. This was an understatement so arresting that I used it in her eulogy and got a laugh, since saying that my mother was never afraid to speak her mind was a little like saying that Joe Stalin was willing to take charge of things.

When agitated, my mother was something to behold, and she was almost always agitated. She had a voice that could knock squirrels from trees. When I was in fifth grade a boy who lived *two streets away* told me on the bus to school that he'd heard me being disciplined the night before.

Ours was not one of those families in which tensions were played out in subtle gestures. My parents fought so much when I was growing up that when no one was yelling in the house I found myself wondering if someone had died. My brother and I didn't have a lot of advanced training in the area, but even we could sense that as far as our parents' emotional lives went, there were certain compatibility and empathy issues that were not being properly addressed.

And yet my parents managed to convey to us that we were their first priority and the objects of their fiercest devotion. And that while they were keenly aware of their own shortcomings when it came to home-building, they had no doubts whatsoever about the paramount importance of the project itself.

Home, in other words, when I was growing up meant all sorts of colliding notions, some of them unsettling and some deeply comforting. Home was that place you went where the love and support might not have been entirely unconditional, but it *was* at least the default position. Where the notion of caring for someone else as a primary value held the most sway.

The grueling year of 2020 and everything it spawned or accelerated has made clear that that primary value of caring for others has never been more important, and put under more pressure. All of the inequities and injustices we've allowed to stand have been wildly magnified, with frequently apocalyptic results.

The apocalyptic, remember—as opposed to the simply catastrophic—carries with it a component of revelation, which almost always implies divine judgment: the reminder that we have brought this upon ourselves, through the ease with which we make room for all of those who marginalize and destroy other human beings. Home and family as concepts are both our potential training ground when it comes to what we imagine to be the necessary acquisition of compassion and empathy and community spirit, and our justification for the opposite: Rudolf Höss, commandant of Auschwitz, by all accounts considered himself a good man mostly because of his efforts to be a doting father and husband.

But it's that first, more benevolent role for family that's the more powerful, I think. I'm as political as I am, when it comes to advocating for others, *because* of my wife, Karen; my sons, Aidan and Emmett; and my daughter, Lucy: *because* of how much being a part of that mini-collective we call the Shepards has instilled in me the reflex to defer my priorities in the face of theirs. When I think about the necessity of making the world a safer or more benevolent place, I think: *for them*.

The year 2020 has also forced on nearly everyone a recognition that usually only accompanies growing old: the understanding that loss is the seminar in which we're all going to be enrolled. The collective version of that understanding, as far as the twenty-first century is concerned, is that calamity is the seminar in which we're all going to be enrolled. In other words, we all have more Chernobyls and Deepwater Horizons and Covid-19s ahead of us. And while those disasters we help create will only exacerbate that tendency we have to see the rest of the world as extras, we have to continue to resist that growing impetus toward devaluing compassion.

And if it seems like a quixotic attempt to keep hope alive in a hopeless situation, well, that may be our task, and it's worked before. It may require a willingness to register that failure might equal, or lead to, success—as Samuel Beckett put it, "So you fail. No matter. Try again. Fail again. Fail better."—and it may require a reconceptualization of the extent to which the smallest individual gestures might interconnect. Belief in ourselves matters, because, as has been proven in the past, we *have* been up to the task of saving one another. And in fact, disaster might be the opportunity that shows us that we *can* be who we hope to be.

My mother was what we used to call a Force of Nature. She was a continual reminder not to do things halfway. When she wasn't whacking at us with wooden spoons or screaming at us, she was hugely loving. And for all of the battering we took, we were unbelievably lucky to have been in the track of her storm. We called her Hurricane Ida. And wherever she passed, there might be downed branches and leaves all over the place, but when the rain stopped, the clouds were washed and beautiful, and the sky was gorgeously clear.

JAMIE DRAKE

Food Insecurity Is Not an Illusion

The reality of hunger in America is greater than ever. More than 11 million children live in food insecure homes, and it is projected that this number could increase to 18 million in 2021. I imagine many of these kids go to bed dreaming of food, and so I created an apparition, a ghost of sustenance. No Kid Hungry can turn these ghosts into reality.

PHOTOGRAPH BY BRITTANY AMBRIDGE

121

JOAN JULIET BUCK

Home?

A HOUSE BY A CANYON, three hotels, two boardinghouses, a pavilion, a villa, a palace, three floors of an *hôtel particulier*, then London: a flat, a mews house, another mews house, a ground-and-lower-ground flat, half a Georgian house, then, by 1980, twelve addresses of my own, and for my parents, a former embassy followed by a bijou apartment, before we all went home to fill in the outlines of their memory of America.

Home is an idea held in place by relics from the journeys, proof of time spent spending money: objects, paintings, carpets, hard furniture. Only force or fire can destroy hard objects. Textiles endure intact, barring an invasion of moths. Rugs can be rolled up and unrolled to cover almost anything, but sofas and soft chairs have only one trick apiece, and inevitably return from the upholsterer with their character impaired.

Home is not walls and ceilings, pipes and roofs, flower beds and front doors. It's as fluid as sand. Home is a packable thing: the objects and paintings wrapped, textiles folded, papers and books stacked.

It's secret stuff in mute boxes, weight for the movers, volume for the storage units. Storage is a vital part of home. Just as secondary characters give life and subplots to drama, you need a crowd of adjunct, accessory, non-central things to animate your places. But the crowd must change or it will become heavy, and possibly crush you.

This is why many objects must be locked up in storage, to be opened up and let out again years later, reborn, as if new. All the better for not being new: known, yet fresh. It's the nomad's trick to keep the senses alert, even in the supposed safety of private surroundings.

I have moved so many times that even when I'm not moving, I move the furniture, the books, the bookcases, the pictures, and the rugs. One wall suddenly looks too emotive, a room needs to be a hug, a table and chairs emit too much brown woodness, things cringe when they should breathe. Vistas must open up, even and especially inside.

Configuration is the key: the relationship between the desk and whatever the sofa is, between the bookcase and the three blue vases, and on just what surface the Colima puppy, sole survivor of the earthquake of '94, should be placed.

I don't envy grand houses I have seen; I envy the person whose desk is placed behind a sofa (though a room with three French windows into a garden would be nice) because the relationship between the desk and the back of the sofa is maximum trust and intimacy. You are working, you could be napping, you could be watching something entertaining, you are tensed and attentive but the possibility of being loose and floppy is right there, and because it's in front of you and not in another room, you don't have to indulge it, you can go on working.

Always keep your eye on the possibility of doing something else. Nomad thinking.

The praying wooden figure stands on the crest of a bookcase in my current shack, as it stood by the window on Beverly Crest Drive, behind the sofa on Chester Street, on the mantelpiece in Paris, on the table in Santa Fe, as blankly beatific as it was the day it was carved four centuries ago in the Netherlands. Its benevolence makes it too gentle for the living room, where it might not tame all strangers, but it's too fervent for the bedroom, where prayer isn't the only thing. It is best placed high up, but not too high, in the privacy of the room where I work, and for obscure reasons of morphic resonance, to my right.

Every object has a charge: mana, mojo, energies, will, intent; or superstition, animism, magical thinking.

Home is where the mojos gather. Sometimes they conflict, and it's up to me to keep the peace. If they're not at peace, I'm not at home. Which may be why I have to keep moving.

JOHN CHARLES THOMAS

I was at a board meeting in New York. Someone at the meeting talked about how much she loved a home she had built in the Colorado Rockies. She said that her "soul lived there." I wrote down those words. Later that night at dinner, I thought again about the conversation from earlier in the day and wrote these words.

Where Lives The Soul

The Soul can wither and leave us bare
With spirit wrung dry, we dare not care
A withered soul robs us of hope
When beaten and worn we shrivel and grope

Our souls seek revival, a place to soar
To climb above the benumbing roar
Our souls crave a place to come alive
A place to fly, to love, to thrive

'Tis not easy to find a home for the soul
We can quest and seek and still come up cold
But for a few, the search bears fruit
By Grace they get a glimpse of truth

They look out upon the boundless plain
And shout and know what they have attained
They stand and proclaim to heaven above
"My Soul Lives Here!" This place I love

And as the gentle Breezes blow
They take Peace from the truth they know
They feel joy as they walk these mortal shores
And all because their Souls found home.

HUNT SLONEM

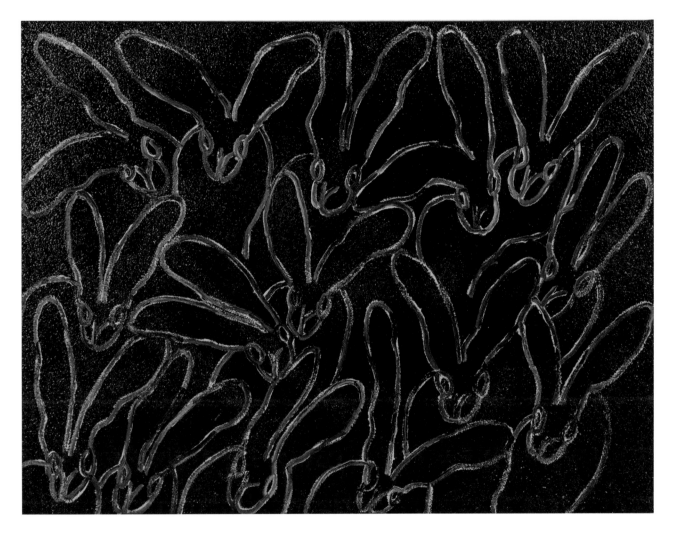

REGINES BLACK DIAMOND, 2020
OIL AND ACRYLIC WITH DIAMOND DUST ON CANVAS

This painting signifies home to me because of its relation to family. The bunnies have a strong connection to each other, and the composition reflects warmth, love, and protection because of the relationship of the bunnies and the ground on which they are painted. The bright texture that emanates from the diamond-dust surface is both inviting and striking, and the bunnies form a strong bond between each other and their environment of home.

IRVING PENN

Love Letter to a Farm

Lisa Fonssagrives-Penn
riding her Tennessee
walking horse on a fall day
when the branches were
abruptly bare, the grass
frozen, the winter closing in.

Vogue, August 15, 1963

127

GABRIELLA
IMPERATORI-PENN

*HOME IS WHERE NATURE IS IN
HARMONY WITH HUMANITY*
FROM A SERIES OF PHOTOGRAPHIC
COLLAGES, 2019

JON MEACHAM

HEN I WAS YOUNG—probably twelve, maybe thirteen—I fell in love. The object of my affection? Robert Penn Warren's *All the King's Men*, which I read and re-read in my grandparents' house on Missionary Ridge, the old Civil War battlefield overlooking Chattanooga, Tennessee. And so when I think of "home," I tend to think of those two things: the book I read, and the house in which I read it.

That dichotomy—I think that's the right word—has shaped my sense of place and belonging ever since. There is the world of the imagination, be it literary or historical, and there is the tangible world of the houses in which I've lived. Chattanooga, Sewanee, Washington, New York, Nashville: Those are my postage stamps of geography. Books formed my first emotional infrastructure, followed, in due course, by my wife and my children. When we were thinking of moving from New York, where our children had been born, back to Tennessee, we got a great piece of counsel from a friend and priest: Your family, he said, is your home.

He was right. My life is unimaginable without my wife and children; genuinely *unimaginable*, for in them and with them I find all meaning and all moment.

Home is also where my books are, for books are a perennial passport to heart and mind. They transcend place, making a home that, like Brigadoon or Trollope's Barchester, knows no geographic boundaries. In the last pages of Warren's novel, Jack Burden, the book's tortured but redeemed narrator, says: "We shall come back, no doubt, to walk down the Row and watch young people on the tennis courts by the clump of mimosas and walk down the beach by the bay, where the diving floats lift gently in the sun, and on out to the pine grove, where the needles thick on the ground will deaden the footfall so that we shall move among the trees as soundlessly as smoke. But that will be a long time from now, and soon now we shall go out of the house and go into the convulsion of the world, out of history into history and the awful responsibility of Time."

For him, home was love, and hope, and history. I know what he meant.

MICHAEL JAMES O'BRIEN *and* ZOLTAN GERLICZKI

HOME IS WHERE THE DOGS ARE: LOLA AND PAULINA, PROVINCETOWN, MASSACHUSETTS, SUMMER 2000

Our dogs were adopted in 1998 from the Humane Society of New York. They lived/traveled with us in New York City, Bellport, Provincetown, Paris, Nice, Tuscany, Milan, and finally to Spain in 2012. Their ashes are scattered off the coast, near Tarifa, where the Atlantic meets the Mediterranean.

JEFFREY BANKS

*H*OME IS MUCH MORE than just a physical place. Home is a state of mind. It's a warm sheltering place you know you can go to anytime and anywhere you are in the world, just by thinking about it. It's sensory overload; full of smells, feelings, and memories, some fraught with joy and some with poignancy.

Home is a place you long for when you are far away and revel in when you are back. It changes throughout your lifetime: what you perceive as Home as a child is different when you are a teenager and far different, again, as an adult, but it is still Home.

Home is a safe refuge that will protect you when the world wages war against you. It also fortifies you when you have to fight your battles after you leave it.

Home is a literal as well as a visceral place. It is a place you can return to just by closing your eyes and willing yourself to it.

Home is the smell of sage and cornbread stuffing or Mother's freshly baked apple pie cooling on a wire rack, or the unmistakable scent of Grandma's dusting powder, or just that vanilla-scented candle eternally burning in the bathroom.

Home is an idea of the mind that is not necessarily made up of blood relatives, but often by the friends of our own choosing—our chosen family, if you will.

Home is the foundation from which so much of our being springs, be it good or bad. So often we think of Home as a structure made of bricks and mortar, but it is oh so much more than that.

Home is the great source of our nourishment as spiritual beings and human souls.

Home is a shelter, deep to the heart.

COREY DAMEN JENKINS

For all of the sheer destructive force that is a churning hurricane, one can actually find a relative sense of peace at its core. In my view, one's home should similarly be a respite from life's storms. Home should be a refuge from daily pressures—a haven where one can be treated lovingly, respectfully, and with the utmost dignity. Home is a chamber for centering, for recharging, for regaining gravity. Home means calm.

PHOTOGRAPH BY WERNER STRAUBE

JULIAN FELLOWES

Y MOTHER WAS VERY GOOD at Christmas. This, I know, can be a source of some irritation to my darling wife and I am sorry for it. I have often told her that she doesn't have to compete with the memory of my late parent when it comes to either cooking or dressing, in both of which Emma effortlessly leads the field, but when it comes to Christmas, I am afraid I must hand the bays to my Mama.

Quite what makes a good Christmas is hard to say, of course. That mixture of the traditional and the novel, that balance between eating and play, that careful casting of the dramatis personae, are all, as elements, filled with pitfalls, although obviously the setting helps. We lived, for most of my growing-up years, in a fairly large, if architecturally undistinguished, rectory-like house in East Sussex.

It had paneling and open fires and a big hall for the tree and all the other folderol associated with Yuletide and, when the festivities arrived, its bedrooms would be crammed with a mixture of friends and family, old and young, as my mother believed that, unlike birthdays or anniversaries or even New Year's Eve, a successful Christmas can only ever be a group activity, and preferably a large group at that.

My three brothers and I made a fractious basis for any party and I remember she always invited at least one guest who was not especially well known to us. This person would be different every year and would be spending the holiday with us for a variety of reasons, but one semi-stranger was invariably present. Years later, I asked her about this curious detail and she nodded. "It was the only way to make you all behave," she said.

And so Christmas would be played out, according to our own family ritual. Midnight Mass on Christmas Eve, stockings to wake up to in the morning, presents after breakfast, always preceded by singing "Good King Wenceslas" in a sort of conga round the hall—the choice of hymn never varied—and then friends would come in for a drink, which would be followed by a light luncheon. After this, there would be a walk or a film on television and, at about 5 p.m., tea, Christmas cake, and Tree Presents.

These last were, I think I am right in saying, peculiar to my family and grew out of our fury as children that all the giving and receiving was done too soon. Each of us would have a couple of "extra," lesser presents from under the tree, usually of the book or record variety, distributed by my mother, dressed up as Father Christmas.

Looking back, I'm not sure why it was she, and not my father, who undertook this task and donned the costume, but I don't believe he ever attempted it, and my mother was always the one in the red hat and the beard, ho-ho-ho-ing as she dished out the last presents of the day. An unlooked-for result of this curious custom was that my niece, Jessica, then three years old, was once heard to greet the Father Christmas on duty in Harrods with a cheery "Hello, Grandmama," which must have puzzled the amiable out-of-work actor inside the fat suit.

That ritual accomplished, the party repaired upstairs to change into black tie for dinner and, after the feast was consumed and the crackers pulled, still wearing those terrifying paper hats, we would play "The Game" and then fall contentedly into bed. As a routine, it never varied, but nor did it disappoint.

However, there was one occasion when we missed out a key ingredient, and I suppose the most vivid memory that I have of a childhood Christmas comes from that time. It was Christmas Eve during the Great Freeze of December 1962. I was thirteen and it was, and remains, the coldest winter that I can remember. It so happened that, for some days before, there had been continual and heavy falls of snow and this really was, for once, a completely white Christmas.

We had dined and, at about 11:30 p.m., it was time to set out for our local town of Hailsham and its rather unprepossessing, 1950s church (all the Catholic churches of my childhood seem to have been Nissen huts or modern mistakes) for Midnight Mass. We piled into my father's car, a Rover I think, although, at this distance, I can't be certain, and we started on our skiddy way.

We carefully negotiated the turning at Muddles Green, the beguilingly titled outskirt of the village of Chiddingly where we lived, and, gradually, with some difficulty, made it to the A22 that would take us to our destination. We had, however, got no farther than the little hamlet of Lower Dicker (the names alone seem like something out of *The Famous Five*), when the vehicle began to splutter and cough and, finally, to die. Cursing loudly, my dear but irascible father nosed it onto the hard shoulder and we all climbed out.

The mobile phone existed only in the pages of Dan Dare in those days and there wasn't a telephone box for miles. Even if there had been, the chances of getting some wretched man from the Automobile Association to attend us at nearly midnight on Christmas Eve seemed pretty slim and, at last, my mother made the decision that we would simply have to walk home and deal with the situation the following morning.

And so we set off. It wasn't too long before we had turned away from the main road and what traffic existed, in that comparatively carless world of long ago, was left behind us. We were alone, a family walking home through a silent, moonlit, winter wonderland. We boys were slightly troubled, as we all knew that there would be a serious problem getting to church the following day, partly because the car would not be mended until after Christmas and partly because the ritual of the festival wouldn't easily accommodate such a dramatic break with tradition.

Sensing this and to still our fears that the morrow might be spoiled, my mother suggested that, having missed Mass that night, instead of attending a service that year, we should sing carols as we walked back.

Although a Catholic, as we all were, she had converted from Anglicanism to marry my father in 1935, and although I don't recall that she had any crisis of conscience or regret about this, there is no doubt that, throughout her life, her Savior remained essentially English, without a trace of Rome or anything as uncomfortable as the Old Testament about Him. As a result, the God of my childhood was a sunny, reasonable being, a figure of infinite understanding and impeccable manners, who could be counted on to take a moderate view.

"God wouldn't expect us to go to Church on a day like this," she would say when the rain was lashing down, or, on a later occasion, when told of the new fashion to extend Sunday Mass with strangers' christenings that would inevitably make one late for lunch: "I'm sure God would never approve of that."

Just so, on the evening in question, her benevolent and social Lord came to her aid, assuring her that a chorus of carols would do nicely when it came to the Fellowes family marking His importance on His birthday. I can see the pair of them now, my mother, still a very pretty woman, in a pinkish coat with a high, mink collar and my father in country tweeds, leading the procession, arm in arm.

Together, we sang the inevitable "Wenceslas" (the only carol my father really knew the words to) and "Silent Night" and *"Adeste Fideles"* as we tramped along on the shimmering, crunching snow, staring up at the star-filled night sky behind the glistening trees, and not caring much, I think, if we disturbed the sleep of the country folk past whose houses and cottages we marched, singing at the tops of our voices.

I can't quite explain why I felt so happy at the time, nor why, even after so many years, it still constitutes a golden moment for me, but it does. My parents are both dead now, my childhood home is sold and my brothers long scattered around the globe, leading their busy lives. But that midnight, winter walk on a cold and brilliant Christmas Eve remains one of my best and brightest memories, and I suspect it will do so until my dying day.

WILLIAM ABRANOWICZ

A home is the most personal of things. It protects and comforts us. The best ones stimulate us creatively.

This image was made at the home of Jeffrey Miller, the stylist, and shows a collection of personal objects placed by his highly refined and masterful hand.

JEFFREY'S SHELF, NEW YORK, 2017

KEITH SUMMEROUR

An Oak Leaf Fireback

An ORIGINAL EXPERIENCE IN ARCHITECTURE is a many-folded, dog-eared, and quiet awakening to those who seek such things. It starts for most of us with the "big idea," which is often rooted in a client's wishes (or demands) and results in what many call style or "curb appeal." After a career working in many an architectural style in many a location, my attention has migrated—I am interested in finding a layer of meaning and depth for both client and curator, for one cannot exist without the other, like daylight is to the night.

With this philosophy in mind, I have embarked on a rather small but fun project—the sculpting of a bronze fireback. Historically, firebacks were meant to decorate and to hold the overnight heat inside the firebox of a Rumford fireplace. The bronze plaque I designed is heavily rusticated and was created using my finger and palm to mimic the movement of smoke. The white oak leaf (*Quercus alba*), a symbol of strength and longevity, is also a meaningful part of our client's business, a popular whiskey distillery.

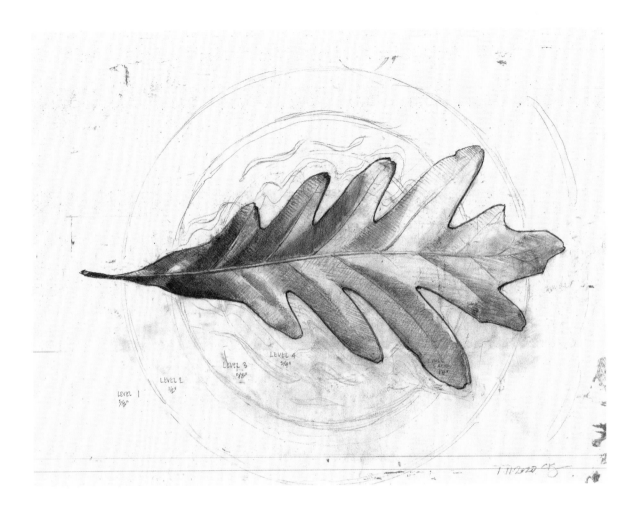

Thus, inspired by a client and sculpted by the architect of their building, the fireback invokes memories each time the flames of a fire interact with the oak leaf.

The process of casting in the lost wax method is an ancient one. It is basic and effective and extremely accurate. First, the clay sculpture is covered in a rubber coating, which creates the mold for the lique-fied wax to be poured into. After the wax solidifies, the rubber mold is removed and the hardened wax is covered in plaster, creating a secondary mold. At this point molten bronze is poured into the plaster cast, which melts and displaces the wax. After chipping away the plaster exoskeleton, the bronze replica is exposed. Various patinas can be applied to the finished product; but knowing the fireback's purpose, I elected for a simple finish because fire would be its eternal, and enhancing, friend.

This first sculpture will not be my last, because I am now inspired to create more detailed and substantial sculptural works. I am always in search of an original experience, and this immersive and inter-active art form achieves that with great excitement!

KEN FULK

F OR ME THERE HAS BEEN no more enduring love of place than Durham Ranch. Fifteen minutes outside of the historic town of St. Helena, California, the seventy-six-acre property is marked by ancient oaks, rocky streams, and a spring-fed pond. It's a former cattle ranch now surrounded by vineyards and olive groves. With little cell phone reception and no Internet connection, it's one of the few places where we can truly escape.

I was charmed by Napa Valley from the beginning, taking frequent day trips soon after we landed in San Francisco. The agrarian history and gentle beauty reminded me of growing up in Virginia. We first lived in a wonderful historic home in the town of Napa that we restored ourselves over a few years. In fact, it was the first house that Kurt and I purchased together, with the help of a loan from his generous father. However, as my business grew and our lives became more and more centered in San Francisco, we reluctantly decided to sell, hoping that one day we'd find another little spot in the country.

As the years went by, I longed for a place where I could disconnect from our hectic life and the dogs could romp and hopefully swim in a pond. One Sunday morning about eleven years ago, while out for a drive in Napa Valley, I came upon the property, and I was instantly enthralled. In fact I still keep the voicemail I left Kurt that day: I kept repeating, "Oh my god, oh my god, oh my god."

The ranch had fallen into complete disrepair and little was left, save the beautiful land, a dilapidated cottage, a cat (soon to be known as Helen), and a chicken (Layla). Initially the thought was to simply "summer camp" the cottage—give it a coat of paint and some furniture, and then someday build a suitable house. Of course this went out the window, and we dove headlong into what amounted to a rebuild from the foundation up. The one thing we were certain of when we began was that we did not want to lose the initial feeling that had drawn us to the place. Nothing fancy, no faux Tuscan retreat or Provençal villa. The inspiration in restoring the property was to pay tribute to the classic California ranch—everything white and stark against the ever-changing landscape. While the concept was based in the traditional, it was important to me that the execution be much more modern. This would help forge a sense of harmony throughout the property, which consisted of a variety of buildings, each with their own distinct appeal.

The original 1940s rancher's cottage was nearly beyond repair, but we did not have the heart to tear it down, despite everyone's advice. It was gutted and rebuilt on the same footprint in the same simple style. The only addition was a large screened-in front porch. The interior was kept classic: bluestone floors (low maintenance and cool for the dogs), board-and-batten walls, and an open rafter ceiling—the only original detail remaining. Fencing from the property was salvaged and used for the cabinetry. Our idea for the barn came a little later, though it is hard to imagine the place without one now. The centerpiece of the property, the barn acts as the social hub, hosting everything from impromptu picnics to spectacular weddings. The 4,000-square-foot structure has thirty-three-foot ceilings and three twelve-by-sixteen-foot steel-and-glass roll-up doors so that everything can flow inside and out. I designed it to one day become the main residence, but we've fallen so in love with this giant cathedral-like space that we can't imagine not having it just the way it is.

The pool—designed primarily for the dogs, with a two-foot bench running the entire forty-five-foot length—was a must. So we added that next to the barn, along with a fire pit, to complete the indoor/outdoor play area. It takes a quick hike up the hill to get to the two year-round tent cabins—our interpretation of guest rooms. We built these as places to stay while we were renovating the cottage, so they are tucked into a wooded knoll overlooking the property and valley. Ironically, they've become the most coveted spots to stay. Oh, and because everyone asks where the ranch got its name: Durham was our first golden retriever. He passed away June 26, 2004. He was the noblest creature I have ever known, man or beast.

PHOTOGRAPH BY VICTORIA PEARSON

CHRISTY TURLINGTON BURNS

Home is where my heart is. It's also where I work, sleep, and meditate, and where I find inspiration most these days. I labored my children here, raised them here.

LEE RADZIWILL

VIOLA, PARIS, 2012
WATERCOLOR PAINTING BY LEE RADZIWILL

Lee Radziwill was famous for many things, including her remarkable beauty, impeccable style, biting wit, and restless, adventurous spirit, all of which I admired in the years in which I counted her as my friend. Lee was also endlessly curious, wanting to know every detail of her friends' lives and constantly seeking out beauty in art, books, fashion, travel, and the natural world. For a few years, she took painting lessons with a teacher in Paris, and from time to time would paint on her own. She never gave much regard to the quality of her watercolors, always botanical in subject, but they were delicate, intimate, and full of charm. They, more than anything else in her homes, make me feel her spirit, her desires, and, poignantly, even her shortcomings. Lee had talent in so many areas, but, as a woman of a certain era and milieu, with many options and perhaps insufficient confidence, she could never muster the fortitude to wholeheartedly devote herself to any of them. And yet, as with all she did or said, these small pictures, made by her hand in private moments, contain a vivid sense of her delightful, inimitable, and original way of being in the world.   —DEBORAH NEEDLEMAN

LESLIE GREENE BOWMAN

What If?

HEN THE CONCEPT of home refers to the iconic estate of Thomas Jefferson, it spins out of orbit into a fascinating intersection of history and culture, revealing, just as do our own domiciles, the public and private, the confident and fragile, the triumphs and the mistakes. But these are writ large at a World Heritage Site. In the home of a founder, they can also reflect the attributes of our culture, our nation, and our own collective psyche.

Monticello was the personal vessel for Jefferson's ambitions, for himself and the nation. The house on the nickel was stunningly aberrant in its time, "the curiosity of the neighborhood"—a Palladian villa with a decidedly French accent in provincial American brick, preposterously and impractically built on a mountain sliced away to become its plinth. The audacity of Jefferson's vision for his home is as breathtaking as his impossible mission statement for thirteen wayward colonies—as if they were remotely capable of winning a war with Britain, much less enacting world-changing ideas of freedom, equality, and the pursuit of happiness. But they did.

Jefferson dared to expose his dreams to the test of reality. Monticello—his opus and autobiography—was perhaps the most personal and vulnerable example. Nearly everything was atypically unprecedented and obsessively intentional, designed to advance Enlightenment ideas of progress and stir the soul with the civilizing power of the arts. He wanted Monticello to challenge and inspire a juvenile nation with a question: "What if?" Were he not revered as a founder we would regard him as a visionary artist, a mad scientist, a magician in his mountain aerie, tinkering with his self-closing French doors, his great clock sounding time across the plantation from a Chinese gong, and a rooftop weather vane that could be "read" from a compass rose on the ceiling of his front porch. What if homes had domes and skylights and parquet floors? What if windows could become doors, beds could disappear into alcoves, and dumbwaiters embedded in fireplace surrounds could mysteriously provide wine from cellars below? Jefferson believed and he dreamed. For posterity he measured his building plans to decimal points beyond the capabilities of a carpenter's rule. What if?

But Monticello was also his crucible of knowledge—for himself and the civilization he believed America must become if it were to take its rightful place on a world stage. He adorned his walls not with family portraits but with an eclectic aristocracy of human knowledge, pairing old world art with new world fossils, a bust of Voltaire with a pre-Columbian figure, a classical sculpture of Ariadne reclining near a wall of Native American artifacts from the Lewis & Clark expedition, all just steps from the greatest library on the North American continent. Everything he created at Monticello drew from the wellspring of that library. But when the British burned the Capitol in 1814, Jefferson offered it to replace that which was lost, for cents on the dollar. Jefferson dared to dream, "What if?" So was born the greatest library in the world.

And in stark contrast to the soaring dreams and ambitions of Monticello, within yards from Jefferson's bedroom windows, is Mulberry Row, lined with humble log and daub slave dwellings and workshops. At home, he could not answer the question he posed in the Declaration—what if all men were created equal? His ambitions for Monticello, and dare we say the survival of a nation, depended on slavery.

PHOTOGRAPH BY MIGUEL FLORES-VIANNA

SUSIE ORMAN SCHNALL

*I*T IS A TRUISM and a fantasy, a rumor and a regret. That we should live not only in houses and apartments and domiciles of all types. But also . . . homes.

Places where there is love. Where the walls have absorbed the smells of cooking, the screams of babies, the silence of prayers. And the secrets of all the inhabitants who have lived there since its front door was first opened to the blossoming young couple or the crumpled widower or the joyous woman spreading her wings alone for the first time in her life.

Places where boys and girls have grown into teens and then into young men and women with big plans and untested desires and glorious potential. Where sleeping babies are looked upon by parents filled with hope and heartbreaking adoration and regrets of what their own lives didn't turn out to be.

Places where carpets are freshly laid or show signs of wear, edges curling, pathways delineated from years of footprints, bare and otherwise, perhaps from soccer cleats, stilettos, work boots.

Places where kitchens have been packed corner to corner with Thanksgiving cooks chopping pecans and stirring potatoes. Where the coffee can practically brew itself. Where pantries have been stacked neatly in store-bought bins with cursive labels or stripped bare during times no one wants to remember yet no one can forget.

Places where living rooms have hosted parties. Where there are indentations on sofa cushions, crumbs and coins hidden underneath. Where an old chair sits, its inhabitant staring at the television. Perhaps a ghost chair. Its inhabitant's ashes sitting on the wooden mantel across the room.

Places where stairways have seen lines of tuxedos and gowns preening for pre-prom photos. Where children have slid atop slippery blankets, bumping and falling and laughing all the way. Where a baby learned to go up and a puppy learned to go down. Where a Christmas tree was hugged by a banister's curve.

Places where bedrooms have witnessed love beginning, thriving, struggling, and ending. Have had their walls covered with idols and trophies and photos and sometimes even holes borne of angry nights. Where pillows have been kissed, tear soaked, and the resting place of a tired head with active dreams that led to rested mornings or sweat-soaked outbursts late in the night. Where memories are held. Never to be shared or forgotten.

Where many dreams have been deferred and denied and discarded. And where other dreams, the lucky ones, have been embraced and embarked upon.

Also, where heartache and worry and sadness have been harbored. For long days and long years. Where corners become classrooms and where closets become conference rooms and places to cry when the tears need to be alone. Where bills and dishes and rugs pile.

Places where fights have been loud, and songs have been sung. Where families have grown with births and marriage and also made smaller by death or leaving. Where new memories are made by each new inhabitant. Where the setting remains the same, but the experiences differ based upon whose singular experience it is.

So what is home? It is where joy is. Where love is. Where promise is. Where sunshine and moonlight are. It is where your people are. It is where you want it to be. It is what you need it to be. It is. It is.

MARIE-LOUISE SCIÒ

These objects bring me back to a feeling of home. They represent a piece of me, and many of them have traveled the world with me. Home is my son, my music, Italo Calvino's book *Palomar*, Adorno's book *Dissonanze*, an Italian Moka coffee maker, memories of Giorgio and of my family, drawings my son made, and so on and so forth. Home is where the heart is, and my heart is with these people and these works of art.

MARTYN LAWRENCE BULLARD

*H*OME IS MUCH MORE than just an address; it is the place that captures your heart, that welcomes you with open arms, cuddles you within its comforts and serves as a sanctuary that relaxes, revives, and restores. For a designer, it is also our experiment pad, a place to trial our decorative fantasies, to juggle color and texture, shape and form and create with design abandon. Spaces to enjoy with friends and family and to enhance and exhibit your talents. Above all, however, for me, the essence of my home is my beloved dog, a soft-coated wheaten terrier named Daisy. The bounding, limitless joy that exudes from our pets is the ultimate tonic; no matter how hard of a day we may have, that welcome home is the most invigorating and delicious moment. Daisy seems to have a built-in clock and knows when to expect me home. She sits staring out of the window wagging her tail until I unlock the door, upon which she springs with all her might toward me, tap-dancing her paws in twirling circles, pounding me with a passion of licks and sparkling eyes. This is the meaning of home, translated very easily into the thing that we all need and strive for, the embrace of unconditional love.

Daisy with her back to the front door entry courtyard of my Palm Springs home, her usual spot from which she launches her loving welcome.

PHOTOGRAPH BY TIM STREET-PORTER

MATTHEW PATRICK SMYTH

Nature is not a place you visit. It is home.
—GARY SNYDER

This quotation sums up what I discovered for myself during this time of confinement.

MELISSA BIGGS BRADLEY

Y HOME IS A CABINET OF CURIOSITIES. Like a crow that flies out into the world and is drawn to shiny objects, I collect talismans and touchstones from my travels and weave them into the rooms of my house. I like to think that I am filling my shelves with "memory triggers" of moments I experienced in far-off lands and also of the friends and road guides who accompanied me, who helped open doorways into new destinations and perspectives.

An ochre-colored, heart-shaped rock from Boynton Canyon in Sedona sits in the drawer of my bedside table, a reminder of the Native Americans who called the towering rock guarding the valley "Kachina Woman," because they saw a female form with a rounded belly in it. In this same canyon, I met a wise healer, and she is the reason I am drawn back to this place on an annual pilgrimage.

Sitting on an eighteenth-century painted Venetian table in my living room is a clenched hand carved in ivory, with the letters "WC" etched in its slender wrist. Once the elegant handle of a washroom, this hand sat in a dusty shop in Beirut. I was with Hoda Baroudi, the Lebanese designer, when I discovered it. Wearing one of her colorful silk robes, Hoda was showing me her city, pointing out inlaid Syrian tables and Persian tiles in a cluttered bazaar. Outside stood facades still bullet-riddled from the city's long civil war, but the ornate gilt clocks and Orientalist watercolors, like my ivory hand, hinted at peaceful, prosperous yesterdays, lost in more modern history.

On another table, a quartz stone, the size of an avocado, sculpted into the shape of a human skull, perches. A shiny *memento mori*, its hollow eyes had caught mine from a basket in a stall in the market in Madagascar's capital of Antananarivo. I had been traveling with two of my closest friends when a flight delay forced an unexpected overnight, so we sought the nearest market to prowl. "Seize the day," the skull reminds me, because our time here is brief—and also, when you are lucky enough to find your kindred spirits, keep them close.

Three ostrich eggs were hauled back in my carry-on from the honeymoon my husband and I went on in South Africa twenty-five years ago. I was drawn to their organic beauty and exotic charm. They sit in a glass bowl atop a bookshelf, having survived three moves, the curious fascination of our children when they were small, and the neglect that comes with being relegated to a high ledge. Despite their fragile form, they have endured and still hold intrigue.

The item I have lived with longest, traveled the shortest distance to me; it is a small porcelain box in the shape of a steam engine with London–NY on its side. My parents met in London, and I imagine one of them found it in an antiques store after they had "crossed the pond" together. They kept it on their mantelpiece when I was growing up. While I love its representation of a kind of dream travel—tracks across the Atlantic—it draws me back to a time when I had yet to board a train or a plane or cross a border. When my pajamas had feet and the engine's tantalizing toy-like form was out of my reach but already hinted at the mysterious allure of foreign lands.

Though my husband thinks I have brought home enough, I cannot stop amassing treasures—and with finds from near and afar, my home acts as a sprawling, three-dimensional inspiration board, adorned with shards of cherished days and the promise of more discoveries.

RUBEN TOLEDO

HOME for me is the manifestation of HEAVEN
ON EARTH. From our run-down beach
house on CONEY ISLAND to the scruffy, noisy loft
in MIDTOWN, my late wife ISABEL managed
to create such a rich atmosphere of soothing peace
and delightful beauty that HOME to me feels
and looks like HEAVEN ON EARTH. This painting
is my homage to her many talents, the reason why
my HOME is inhabited by so many ISABELs in every
nook and cranny filling HOME with a nurturing,
secure, and radiant spirit—my point of arrival for
dreams and departure of plans.

MARTINA MONDADORI

*T*HERE IS A GERMAN WORD that describes the philosophy behind *Cabana* magazine better than anything else: *gemütlich*. We could translate it as *coziness*, but it is really a bit more broad than that. It's that feeling one has when walking or sitting in a room with a soul. It's really what one feels when being "at home." Capturing the essence of this feeling is what we try to achieve with *Cabana*.

The interiors I love are layered, colorful, and very personal. It takes time to layer, because it takes time to collect and decorate. Decorating a home is like a journey, a bit like life is. You bring in objects, memories, people. Some are there to stay, some are transient. To create an atmosphere—well, that takes more than just decoration and it is that "something" that we look for when choosing which rooms to publish in the magazine. What generates an atmosphere in a room? A certain number of things, but I believe it resides in the combination or, better said, the harmony of them all. The furniture, the way it is displayed. The light (oh the light!). The smells. The objects and the stories that each one tells (to reference Oliver Hoare). The juxtaposition of textures and fabrics. The proportions, which are crucial. The effects certain colors have with the light during the day. Being able to obtain the perfect mix of these ingredients is that art that great decorators, or great aesthetes, have been able to master. I believe it is almost *alchemy*, not science. Certain rules apply, but those rooms that speak to the soul, well, that is a different thing. And in difficult times, these abodes have the power to console, enchant, and heal our souls more than anything else.

ABOVE: PHOTOGRAPH BY MIGUEL FLORES-VIANNA

OPPOSITE: Il Convento Suore Riparatrici, S. Andrea Apostolo dello Ionio.
PHOTOGRAPH BY GUIDO TARONI

MICHAEL HAINEY

*T*HE FIRST PLACE I LIVED in New York City was a boarding house, owned by Quakers. People don't believe me, but it's true. This was the late 1980s, and I'd moved from Chicago to take an internship at a magazine that paid $50 a week. It was an old brownstone in the East Village, dating from the 1840s, and for $300 a month I got a tiny room that came with a loft bed and a desk beneath it. There was a shared bathroom down the hall. A woman cooked breakfast and dinner for the twenty or so of us who called that place home, and we shared our meals at a communal table. The first night I slept there, I laid in my bed and looked at the ceiling and felt I was the luckiest person in the world—somehow, I had carved out a small corner of Manhattan. I belonged.

Now I live maybe ten minutes away from that little room, in Greenwich Village, just off of Fifth Avenue. I live with my wife, Brooke, in an apartment that, thirty years ago, I could have only dreamed I would own. We are fortunate—during those early days of that long spring of 2020, our home was a small haven in which to isolate as the coronavirus ravaged the city we love. We have a view that's pretty similar to what Jimmy Stewart had in *Rear Window* (which was set a block away from where we live): we get to gaze onto gardens of other brownstones. It brought calm, especially watching spring bring it all to life. I even hung a bird feeder off our fire escape. A few days after I did, we had a downy woodpecker stop by, his shock of red feathers atop his head fluttering in the wind as he pecked away. Who knew there are woodpeckers in Manhattan? In the stillness of the city, new characters took the stage.

Most of the time during lockdown, I wrote. Trying to create in those days something new and worth remembering. There is a screenplay of my first book, while I also work on the sequel to that book. After about two weeks indoors, we started to venture out, for walks at dawn. Then a short time later, we started to include a walk two or three evenings a week, at 7 p.m., to the hospital down the street, to gather with others and clap for the healthcare workers. One night, as people were starting to gather, a cop came around the corner, mounted on a black horse. He clip-clopped his way into the middle of Seventh Avenue, and stopped the few drivers who were on the street. Just then, I heard the bell on the Jefferson Market library toll 7 p.m. and people began to clap. The healthcare workers, gowned in green and masked in blue, came out. And just then, too, a truck with giant speakers pulled up, blaring "New York, New York," by Frank Sinatra. I know it sounds schmaltzy. Maybe like something out of a movie. And maybe it should, because what else is life in New York but a movie, with incredible highs and heartbreaking lows? We stood there, all of us, masked and clapping, listening to the music, to Sinatra's voice, to his words, pushing us on, lifting us up. "*I want to be a part of it . . . I'm gonna make a brand new start of it . . .*" It had all the energy of a game-seven, rally-in-the-late-innings, Yankees win. The old lady next to me, white-haired and thin as an egret, took her cane and started banging it against a battered garbage can—*Clang! Clang! Clang!* The energy among us built and built. And then Sinatra finished and all of us—the crowd, the healthcare workers—let out a whoop. I heard a horse whinny, and I looked and there was the mounted cop, his horse rearing up on two legs in the middle of Seventh Avenue. I turned for the first time to look at Brooke. I had avoided looking at her because I knew if I did, I would weep. And we did weep. Two masked faces, only our tear-filled eyes visible. Happy tears. I said to her, "I love this filthy fucking city. Nothing can break us. There is nowhere else I'd rather be."

"Me, neither," she said.

It's the spirit of New York. It's eight million people, but the strength and power and joy of it comes from the people who choose to live here. That night, back in our home, when I lay in bed with my wife, I felt the same way I did my first night in Manhattan, at that Quaker boarding house. Happy. And that I was the luckiest person in the world.

We're going to be all right. All of us.

KITTY HAWKS

How THE HAWKS' NEST became THE DOGS' HOUSE

I have loved dogs all my life and am especially partial to rescues. My husband and
I have adopted seven since we moved here. We usually think of our dogs as pets, but our
latest has shifted the paradigm: we are his humans.

LARRY LEDERMAN

Mornings and evenings give pure
joy while we sit in this garden
watching the bees move like breezes
through the nepeta and the roses.

SUSAN WISSLER

"NO ONE FULLY KNOWS our Edith who hasn't seen her in the act of creating a habitation for herself," claimed Edith Wharton's close friend and fellow novelist, Henry James. Her houses were extensions of herself, displaying her taste, values, and character. Wharton, in her own words, was "unafraid of change, insatiable in intellectual curiosity, interested in big things, and happy in small ways." These characteristics are reflected in her homes.

She published her first book, *The Decoration of Houses*, in 1897. It was inspired by renovating her home in Newport, Rhode Island, which she called "an ugly wooden house with half an acre of rock." One of the book's guiding principles is that "it is essential to consider for what purpose the room is to be used." Moreover, "it must not be 'a library,' or 'a drawing-room,' but the library or the drawing-room best suited to the master or mistress of the house which is being decorated." Perhaps because she couldn't quite get her Newport home to "suit" her, four years later, in 1901, she sold it and bought 113 acres in Lenox, Massachusetts. There she would build The Mount, which she would recall in her memoir, *A Backward Glance*, as "my first real home."

She poured herself into every aspect of The Mount's design—it is full of Wharton. Shy by nature, she was exceedingly warm and gracious to friends. The Mount reflects both of these aspects. The front of the house is simple, almost austere, with only two entryways. Yet the back of the house, the side that she shared with her friends, is elegant and open, practically bursting with French doors leading out to the wide, sunny terrace overlooking her gardens. Once inside, first-time visitors are often surprised how livable such a large, initially imposing house can feel.

But while The Mount was Wharton's first real home, it was not her last. In 1911 she separated from, and soon divorced, her husband, putting an entire ocean between them by moving to Paris. When the First World War broke out, she started several charities to aid the Allies. She also edited *The Book of the Homeless*, an anthology of pieces from writers and artists such as Yeats, Stravinsky, and Renoir to raise funds for wartime refugees. Exhausted at war's end, she bought a house north of Paris, the Pavillon Colombe, and another in the south of France called Château Sainte-Claire. She loved both homes, but Sainte-Claire, she declared, was her "Great Good Place" and its garden "just pure *heaven*!"

"The Great Good Place" is a short story by Henry James about a harried author who, in a dream, visits somewhere—a convent? a hotel? it's never clear—where he is completely and utterly at peace. After the First World War, one can imagine why such a place would appeal to Wharton. Fortunately, hers actually existed.

Situated on a hillside overlooking the Mediterranean in the French Riviera town of Hyères, it's easy to understand why Wharton loved, and felt at home in, Sainte-Claire. The house, long abandoned when she moved in, required extensive renovations. She undertook them with gusto. She delighted in establishing grand, terraced gardens, finding that "to a gardener accustomed to the rigours of New England, it is like a dream to be planting out camellias, cypresses, & every known rose."

Hyères became the favorite place for her friends to visit. Of her first Christmas at Sainte-Claire, she wrote that "yesterday was the happiest Xmas I have spent in many a long year. I can wish no old woman of my age a better one!" Those happy Christmases would continue, as it became a tradition for several friends to join Wharton at Sainte-Claire for the holiday, reading to one another and enjoying Christmas pudding. It's no wonder she declared that "It is good to grow old—as well as die—'in beauty'; & the beauty of this little place is inexhaustible."

Wharton's novels often portray how people are shaped by, and in turn shape, their places. In her stories, the cost of not fitting in can be tragically high. It's a struggle she felt living in America, as she was seen as too fashionable for Boston and too intellectual for New York. In France, and in Hyères particularly, there was no such conflict. At Sainte-Claire, she could be both. May we all find our Great Good Place.

PHOTOGRAPH BY RICHARD POWERS

Putting small things together in unexpected ways can turn a collage,
or a room, into a pleasant, personal surprise.

MITCHELL OWENS

ROOMS ARE WHERE our past and present come together and await our future. They are where we wake and where we sleep, where we make love, where we argue and pout, where we bring up children, where we experience the humdrum as well as the transcendent, and very often, most often, where we die. A room is the first thing most of us ever see and often the very last.

The best ones tell us about who we are, what we need, what we're avoiding, and sometimes hint at where we are going. This is true whether it's a restaurant or a school or an office or a children's ward in a hospital or a dentist's waiting room or a dining room intended for the mythical married couple with 2.5 children. This is the reason why an architect I know presents his students with a reading list that has nothing to do with the professions of architecture or interior design. So off they go, puzzled perhaps, clutching that seemingly inexplicable roll call of the novels of Honoré de Balzac and Edith Wharton, of the journals of the Goncourt brothers, of the poems of Matthew Gregory, the plays of Tennessee Williams, and more, literary works in which rooms, meticulously observed and atmospherically described, are characters in themselves but, more importantly, that embody, figuratively and literally, their inhabitants— rooms that are, in a way, mirrors. Speaking of Williams, in his play *A Streetcar Named Desire*, Blanche DuBois covers a naked light bulb with a cheap paper lantern for a reason.

As a writer and an editor, and simply as a curious person, I look at rooms with an intense desire to read them, like a fortune-teller does tea leaves: Why that lamp, why that table, why that tile, why that mantel, why limestone instead of marble, why *that*? What explanations hide beneath the surface? Is the room a calculated escape, a reaction against something? Or is it an embrace? What does it say about the designer or the architect or the client or even our moment in time?

In 1960 Solange d'Ayen, a French duchess who served as the editor in chief of French *Vogue* as well as French *House & Garden*, was asked why Paris decorators turned out so many eighteenth-century-style interiors in the decade after the Second World War. Her answer was simple and affecting, describing postwar France as "a country that was barely breathing" and explaining that in order for it to regain its health, the nation found strength in the glory of its past. A cigar may indeed be just a cigar, someone supposedly once said, but all of us know that a Louis XVI chair carved by hand in the Atomic Era is much, much more than a pretty replica. "It is only shallow people who do not judge by appearances," Oscar Wilde, long ago, observed. "The true mystery of the world is the visible, not the invisible."

What I'm trying to say is that every room we create has resonance. My daughter once complained to me, in a conversation I'd rather forget, about furnishing our living room, "Why does everything in this house have to be about style?" After my initial shock that my own child would question the importance of style, that she found it superficial and somewhat silly, I explained that design shapes and reflects our lives in many ways; it melds history, memory, lessons, hopes, aspirations, dreams. The living room you decorate, the hotel lobby you conceive, the table that is made by a craftsman under your supervision: everything you create contains a story, a story that is ultimately part of a bigger, broader story, one that will eventually come into contact with those unseen, unknown individuals who will interact with your projects long after you've completed them and moved on to another commission.

MARGOT SHAW

ACCORDING TO Merriam-Webster, *home* is defined as "one's place of residence." What a prosaic and bare-bones definition! So literal.

When I consider the word *home*, I begin to dream, imagine, roll it around in my mind like a many-faceted stone. Words and pictures from my archives come up, like Simon and Garfunkel's iconic lyrics "Home, where my thought's escaping, home where my music's playing, home where my love lies waiting silently for me"; home free—being either close to or having successfully completed something and sensing the joy and relief of it; homesick, that wistful longing for our familiar, comfortable place; and as a 'Bama native, "Sweet Home Alabama"— though the anthem is a bit rough-and-tumble, those opening chords still bring a smile.

But the most poignant usage of home in my canon comes to mind periodically over the years and still brings a pang of deep regret: my daughter, a child of divorce from the age of three, has grown into an incredibly brave, smart, empathetic, and successful human being. However, from her first days of school, whenever she would suffer some pain, either from a friendship gone awry, a hurtful word spoken by a peer, the disappointment of being excluded, or even a loss in sports, if she let herself really feel the hurt and begin to cry, she would often howl, "I want to go home."

I puzzled over this phrase for a good long while, 'til one day, when I was apparently ready, heart and soul, to know and understand this plaintive expression, it was revealed. Home, to my daughter, was partly the tiny starter house where she arrived from the hospital; where she was strolled in the sunshine; where she lived blissfully and safe, playing with a lovable Lab named Otis and playdate mates; and where she was loved and cherished, day in and day out by her parents. Until it all broke . . . Home was the feeling of wholeness and security of life.

I had imagined and witnessed the sadness my divorce caused in my daughter, but on that day when I finally grasped the depth of her sorrow, I remember whispering to myself, "I want to go home too."

PHOTOGRAPH BY CLAIRE TAKACS

MIGUEL FLORES-VIANNA

PALMYRA, JANUARY 7, 2011

Since the dawn of time, for millions
of people, the idea of home has only been
the memory of what was left behind.

MICHAEL IMBER

Margaret

My father's sister, my Aunt Margaret, my godmother,
was an artist. A watercolorist. As a child I'd explore
her home, full of interesting objects and flowers,
mostly orchids. She loved to paint orchids. Her house
sat at the end of Old Galveston Highway. Its ancient
wooden bridge long gone, it was just an abandoned
oyster-shell road through a swamp. She would take
me on walks down this road, through the dark woods.
She would point out every detail, every moss-hung
cypress, every turtle, every bird, every orchid.
She taught me to see. Eventually, she taught me
to paint. But first, I had to see.

My Aunt has long since passed and I still paint.
I painted these flowers for my daughter, Sari.
So that she may see what Margaret saw.

NICHOLAS BENSON

THE TWENTIETH CENTURY saw a tremendous shift in human societal and economic structure. With the advent and application of mass production on a vast scale after the Second World War, the average human's connection to the physical world—the way in which we could produce a variety of things with our own hands—diminished. Particularly in the United States, the idea of making money for money's sake became a driving force that supplanted the philosophy at the heart of our simple motto "Made in America."

Processes in refining and accelerating the efficiency of our societal structures led to digital technology. As much as this evolution has been an unarguably beneficial leap it has also brought deeper philosophical questions about the nature of human interaction. Mass media and the onslaught of information, which is not only accessible but often unavoidable, have left us wondering who we are and what we want of ourselves and our country. This can be seen so clearly today in racial conflict, economic inequality, and even insurrection. If John and Joan Q. Public are desperately scratching away to earn a barely livable wage, how are their children faring?

I choose to use my age-old craft (stone carving, a practice that is as old as humanity itself) as a symbol of human history, and I set it in conflict with the nature of digital information—information that often lasts for only a nanosecond. I hope to immediately provoke questions for the viewer. What does it say? What does it mean? Who are we? Where are we going?!

This outlook is not all bleak. It also speaks to the capacity of the human mind. Digital technology is an amazing achievement. Look what we can do when we set our minds to it. Can we change the things that we must?

18-MILLION (DETAIL), 2020
CARVED NATURAL-SPLIT SLATE

JEREMIAH BRENT *and* NATE BERKUS

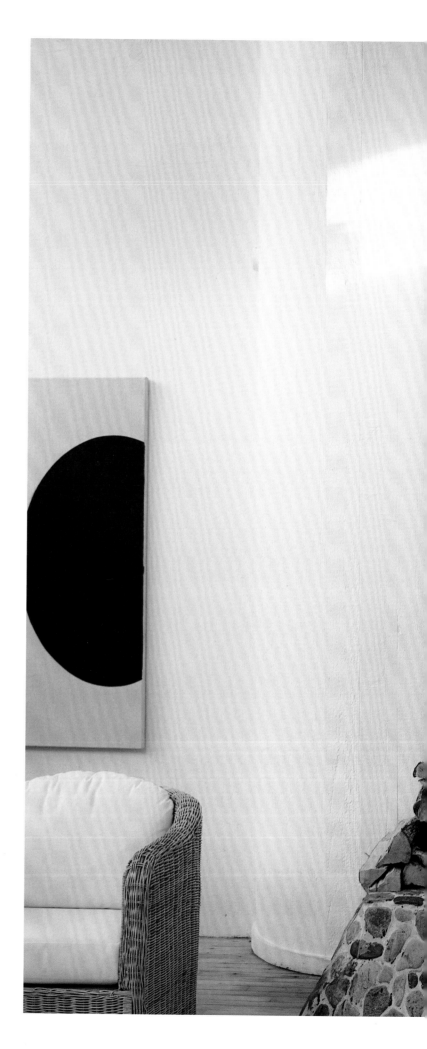

Home, to us, is where you tell your story—every chapter unfolds as your eye travels around the room. This philosophy guides how we approach interior design for ourselves and our clients, and over time the space becomes infinitely layered as the memories and meanings deepen. For example: this collection of Peruvian clay bulls, or *Torito de Pucará*, which are typically given as gifts and placed on the roof for good luck, remind us of our engagement at Machu Picchu—the trip that really established our commitment to each other and the commencement of a new life together.

A collection of clay bulls on a stone fireplace at the Montauk house of Brent and Berkus

PHOTOGRAPH BY LAURYN TUMPKIN

THOMAS A. KLIGERMAN

Home is familiar; it is the place that comforts you, where your heart is. In my travels I am always taken by the pride people have in their countryside, their villages, towns, cities and, maybe most important to me as an architect, their buildings. I painted this view of the Taj Mahal from within the deep red sandstone vestibule of the neighboring mosque. I was struck by the quiet reverence those gathered showed toward the gleaming marble Taj. I had traveled halfway around the planet to see this architectural icon and extraordinary wonder of the world. To the Indians gathered there that day, it was home.

KELLY WEARSTLER

Our homes tell stories about us. The ways we choose to utilize and decorate the places we inhabit paint pictures of our personalities, offering unique insights into our minds and hearts.

Designing a home is so personal, and requires a deep understanding of how to meet and celebrate the individual needs of those who live there. For example, a hidden bar tucked under the staircase of a Manhattan residence reveals that the occupants are avid entertainers, who love to surprise and delight their guests. It's quirks and idiosyncrasies like this that turn a collection of spaces into a home.

OBERTO GILI

Home is where dreams, love, nature, and passion interact together.

PAMELA FIORI

HEN MY HUSBAND, COLT—the love of my life—died in 2020, I had the epic task of going through his eighty-one years of "keepsaking" (some might call it hoarding). We were married for thirty-eight years; together for forty. But long before meeting me, he saved every meaningful memento: snapshots of himself as a little boy, family Christmas cards, his father's collection of pipes, and his mother's poetry. As an adult, during a long and successful career as a creative director in advertising and as a freelance graphic designer, he filled flat files, boxes, and albums to the brim with samples of his work, sketches, and photos. He kept vintage issues of *Life* and *Time* magazines from the Second World War era, award plaques, souvenirs from trips, even articles of clothing that meant something to him—his army uniform, for example, carefully preserved in a garment bag. The first night we got together, long before we became serious about each other, he arrived at my apartment wearing a green Shetland sweater that remains carefully placed in a drawer to this day, as if it were made of gold. He couldn't bear to part with it.

That's the kind of man Colt was: deeply sentimental and hell-bent on memorializing every moment. He was single into his early forties and was accustomed to going to bars with his colleagues for an after-work drink (or two or three). That is, until we got married in 1982. From then on, he wanted to be home. Having a real home, at last, and a wife meant the world to him.

He was also super sentimental about Christmas, maybe because he'd spent so many of them alone in New York. Yes, he had relatives and friends he could visit, but he was still by himself. Not that any of a number of available women wouldn't have jumped at the chance to spend the holidays with such a handsome, unattached Manhattan male in the hope of transforming what seemed to be a confirmed bachelor. But, as it turned out, not a bachelor forever.

On Christmas Eve of 1981 and after we'd been together for a year, we were coming back from visiting my parents in New Jersey. Instead of taking the usual detour to avoid the holiday crowds and midtown traffic, he instead drove directly and with considerable determination to Rockefeller Center. "I want to see the tree." "You'll never get a parking place," said I (sounding like a cynical New Yorker). At that exact moment, a car pulled out from an ideal spot and Colt pulled in. A miracle. We walked over to the prime place for a view of the ever-glorious tree. Suddenly Colt got down on his knee and asked, "Pamela, will you marry me?" Of course, I said yes almost before he finished the proposal. And, by the way, it's not lost on me that had he not gotten that parking space, I might have remained single.

In 2020, as I began unearthing his relics with the zeal of an anthropologist, I came across a slew of interoffice memos, appointment books dating back to the early 1970s, and even some love letters written by women who pursued him (he never pursued them; he never had to). They were usually apologizing for having pushed him for a commitment that he wasn't ready to make.

I also found a trove of his cartoons, which he did for fun, not profit, and are hilariously funny. They lightened my days during what might have been a heartbreaking process. One of the most touching artifacts I came across was a letter that he wrote, presumably to himself, while he was in the US Army, posted in Vitry-le-François, an army base outside of Paris. This was in 1962, perhaps the first time he was that far away from home. Even though Colt served as an MP, there is nothing remotely militant or cool-headed about the tone of the letter. It is tender, all heart and all him.

180

23 DECEMBER,
1962
France, somewhere east of paris.

Christmas, I suppose, has lost its meaning this year. tomorrow is Christmas eve.

OH, I guess I speak of the meaning of Christmas quite selfishly. I think of the comfortably warm home, the smells of the tree, The wreath, the KITCHEN, the rosy red glow That everything assumes this TIME of year. I can vividly recall the way in which christmas affected my senses; the sounds of bells and carrollers, Christmas wrappings, the snow, The sounds of the city busying itself for the few short days. I can remember surrounding myself with all things christmas; walking down Fifth Avenue or Third, standing in Grand Central Station watching the 5:29ers smiling laughing, whispers of Merry CHRistmas, gift wrapped for the days ahead, the early night, a million lights, a million people, Reds, GReens, golds and silver, Blazing store windows, music a bitter cold, warmth and going home.

KELLY MARSHALL

I spend a lot of time in other people's homes.

As an interiors photographer I have been ushered into
spaces I could only have imagined visiting—the grand,
the lavishly decorated, the abandoned, the desired,
the relic, as well as the spaces of the forlorn, the dreamer,
the lover, and the thief.

If you are listening, spaces tell you everything you need
to know about themselves and their inhabitants.

I do my best to honor that permission of access.

But what does home really mean? And how is it supposed
to feel? The concept of home has never really landed
on me, it hides in a corner of my psyche quietly awaiting
some attention. I used to chalk it up to my unconventional
childhood, lack of generational family, and living
in a highly racialized country, but I've always been...

restless.

How can I feel safe and comfortable in a country built
in every way to thwart and deny that endeavor? I inhabit
a violent nation on stolen land built by stolen people and
wonder why I am so...

unsettled.

I've done enough inside work to know my true home is
myself—fully grounded in self-love. It is the feeling of being
enveloped in my husband's arms, the laughter shared
with the best of friends, holding my mother's gaze, and
swimming in the ocean. Home is fortifying and unlimited.

And yet... I continue to knock on your doors and ask to see
what is inside. I am inquisitive about the things we buy
to make ourselves feel safe and on the right side of things.
I continue to unpack how some can have so much
and many more so little and we still sleep so well at night.

NINA CAMPBELL

M<small>Y FATHER AND MOTHER</small> had what was termed Good Taste, and our houses were always comfortable and calm, or at least the color schemes were because my mother was very volatile! I was extremely lucky though, because I realised that Home was a haven, and certain things were sacrosanct. A comfortable and pretty bedroom, with an inviting bed, was as important as a well-laid table and delicious food. The drawing of the curtains in the evening denoted that it was time to relax and entertain friends or just family. We moved house a great deal when I was a child, and I always found this very exciting as it meant a new bedroom and I was always allowed to choose my decorations. I suppose it was my only option to go into the design world.

When I got a job at Colefax and Fowler I really had no idea what an interior designer did, although I had been to a design school for a few months. During my interview I told Mr. Fowler of my education, at the school of a rival, and he said to me, "Please forget everything you learnt there," whereupon I told him I hadn't really learnt anything. He was thrilled with this response and hired me immediately.

I was hopeless at making the tea; on my first day I proudly produced a cup for Mr. Fowler that he described as milk soup, and he begged me never to make tea again. I advanced to bag carrier and as such went with him, walking behind, as he strode across roads, oblivious to traffic, and miraculously we arrived at 44 Berkeley Square. This was a most amazing house, built by William Kent for Lady Isabella Finch in 1744; it had a beautiful double staircase leading to the first-floor drawing room, where the coffered ceiling was a masterpiece, painted in red, blue, and gold. Pevsner considered it to be *the* finest terraced house in England.

John Aspinall had decided to open the most extravagant and exclusive gaming club and had asked John Fowler to restore and design the club, and this was where I was taken on my second day of work! Much later, when I had started my own business, I was asked by Mark Birley to work on the basement of this building, where he had created the legendary Annabel's club. I was so lucky to have my eyes opened to the most extraordinary interiors and houses.

I have always felt very blessed to have chosen this career; it is lovely to create homes for clients and give them their dreams.

Houses can either be grand and imposing, or simple and charming. But whatever they are the only thing that really matters is that they are inviting. Surely the best possible feeling is when we have given friends a good meal, good conversation, and hopefully introduced them to other people who amuse and interest them.

Let us never forget how truly lucky we are to have a home and be able to feed our friends and family.

PHOTOGRAPH BY SIMON BROWN

PAMELA JACCARINO

This interior painting reflects on the Persian proverb: "If you have two pennies, use one to buy bread. With the other, buy a hyacinth for your soul." Beauty, interiors, art, and design have the power to uplift the human spirit.

Pamela Jaccarino '20

WENDY GOODMAN

The Gift

"**I** FOUND SOME PHOTOGRAPHS I think you might be interested in," Richard Avedon said back in 2003 at a chance meeting we had in the hallway of Industria studios, where we were working on separate photo shoots. Then he told me to call his studio and make an appointment so he could show me photographs he had taken during one of his trips to Paris in the 1950s. He also said that he wanted to give them to me because of the subject matter, something that I'd like. I wondered if I had heard that last part correctly, but two days later I was sitting next to him at the picnic table in the little kitchen alcove in his studio where everyone had lunch. He repeated that he was giving me these photographs as a gift, "to do what you want with." He told me that he had been working on his archive, getting rid of lots of things, but this shoot held special meaning for him because the subject was something that he had never done before—an interior. The strips of film, which he carefully withdrew from their paper envelopes, had not even been cut but remained intact, as they had been delivered to him all those decades ago. Strip by strip we examined each image, discolored by age, but even so, otherworldly and extraordinary. "I just wanted to record the most amazing rooms I had ever been in," Dick said, taking me back to his first visit to the apartment of Suzy Delbée and her husband, Pierre Delbée, a director of the legendary French decorating enterprise Maison Jansen. The firm had brilliant workshops where any style of furniture and artisanal treasure could be conjured up, including the five custom doors, created for the Delbées' apartment, made of ebony and inlaid with ivory and bronze that took twenty months to complete. Dick and his wife, Evelyn, would have entered the foyer with its Louis XVI–style paneled walls painted a delicate blue, trimmed in white, and punctuated by those bold doors.

It had started with an invitation. Suzy Delbée had asked Dick and Evelyn to dinner. The request was a complete surprise, because Dick had never met his hosts, but he was captivated when the invitation was delivered in an ostrich egg on a silver platter with a note reading, "I admire your work." Upon arrival, he was so dazzled by this Parisian residence that he felt compelled to capture the magic of the spaces with his Rolleiflex camera. The two couples most probably dined in the foyer, where a gateleg "Royal" table would have been wheeled in, its black surfaces trimmed with gunmetal steel and gold plating, gleaming in the candlelight. The Avedons would have been astounded by the luxury of the sofa covered in real leopard skin and the doors of the library upholstered in a moss-green suede. The photographs were Dick's effort to capture the astounding ambience and decor of this jewel-box apartment on the avenue Foch. They are a fascinating document of how he viewed certain details in the space and how he attempted to get his depiction of them just right. One of the handmade sculptural doorknobs was taken from different angles, multiple times. And, as many exquisite antique pieces of furniture as there were in the opulent rooms, including an Empire ormolu-mounted chair attributed to Georges Jacob, macabre and unexpected elements were what Dick zeroed in on: small, carved-ivory skulls—part of a larger collection of memento mori—on one of the bookshelves in the library; details of the bath accessories in the master bathroom; and the modern flourish of framed sheet music on the walls of a hallway leading to the bedroom. This visit was the beginning of a friendship between the Avedons and the Delbées, who were like mythical characters out of a Proust novel, sparing no extravagance to delight and entertain their brilliant American guests.

PHOTOGRAPH BY RICHARD AVEDON

STAN DIXON

Sitting by the fire at home amongst
family and friends is one of the most
peaceful instances of camaraderie.
At the center of home, the hearth provides
warmth and light, inviting all to gather
in a space of energy and rejuvenation.
As relaxation and inspiration kindle
from the flames, one can find comfort
in the tranquil feeling of "home."

STEELE THOMAS MARCOUX

Growing up, I had the great privilege of spending nearly every weekend with my family at a lake house in the North Georgia mountains. We lived in Atlanta, but our family moved several times while I was a child—my parents never shied away from a new adventure, or decorating project—and after I went away to college in New England, then moved to Washington, DC, to work as a reporter, I stopped thinking of Atlanta as "home." Throughout all that moving around, as my mother says, the lake house was constant. Change, whether to annual traditions like the July Fourth wooden boat parade or to the decorating itself, didn't really happen there, and that was a great source of comfort to me and my sister.

That is, until my parents decided they were ready for one more big adventure: making a permanent move to *their* happy place in Florida when they retired nearly six years ago. Selling the lake house accompanied this decision, and my sister and I were as crushed for ourselves as we were excited for them.

As a sort of consolation prize, my parents gave me a triptych painting by the artist Libby Mathews that depicts the view of the mountains from the lake house. The paintings had hung in our living room there, and now they hang in my dining room in Birmingham, Alabama, where I have been working every day for nearly twelve months. Like so many of us during this difficult year, I've adapted to living with uncertainty and loss—we lost my father to Covid-19 in June. But this majestic view of the lake and the mountains—and all of my associated memories of love, connection, ritual, and joy—has comforted me every day. This vision of home, I've learned, will live forever in my mind and my heart.

PHOTOGRAPH BY HOLLAND WILLIAMS

SETH GODIN

Let's Go Home

BECAUSE IT'S MORE THAN just a house. More than the place where we spent a lot of time. More than an address we know by heart.

Home is a feeling. It's the smell, the sounds, the aura of that place, the one where we know we belong.

For too many, of course, none of this is true. Even if they were fortunate enough to have a house, they were deprived of a home. Instead of a place of respect, dignity, and safety, that house was a risk, a reminder of the instability that they were thrown into, day after day, through no fault of their own.

The caste system of the United States may have amplified that deprivation. It could have been caused by social stress or mental illness. It might be related to misapplied criminal justice or drug abuse. It doesn't really matter, because it happened.

Someone took home away.

And without that foundation, so many other things are hard to imagine or create.

Home is a refuge. For Superman, it's way up in the Arctic, where no one can bother him. For Wonder Woman, it's on a remote island, while the Black Panther has his own country, far away. For the rest of us, home is probably right around the corner, or at least it used to be. That place where the bullies can't find us, where a parent is ready with a hug, a kind word, or a reassuring smile.

It's from foundations like these that we find the strength to imagine what's possible. Because we know that someone has our back, we can visualize a future where we have someone else's back. Because we were treated with respect and given dignity, we know what that looks like and have a hunch that we can offer it to someone else, perhaps even today.

My parents have been gone for a while, but I think of them every day. I think about how hard they tried to make it look easy, how much they cared about creating a home for my sisters and me. Most of all, I think about the standard they set for what was possible. They knew that safety and sufficiency and generosity were contagious, and that it began with them, and then was handed off to us.

What was dinner like for you growing up? Do you remember sitting down as a family, once a week, or perhaps every night? Did you have the expectation that there'd be food, that your parents would serve it without being stressed (or causing you stress)? Was there a conversation around that dinner table that reminded you that you were home, that this was your place, that anything was possible?

Home is where our future begins. It always has. And if we can share that feeling and create that possibility for others, we've opened the door in a way that our parents knew we could.

SIMON WATSON

*I*AM A PHOTOGRAPHER and, not unlike an electron, I am almost always in a constant state of motion, and so probably about half my life has been spent in places that aren't my home. In fact, I am frequently thousands of miles away from it. I love traveling: it has formed me and educated me—I still get giddy when I'm packing my suitcase. But oddly, when I'm away, I think of my home and my life there; I miss it and long to return to it. And so, I think I am happiest at home. It's where I have everything: my family, my belongings, my stuff—the things that I have collected over the course of my life and my many travels. I need my stuff. I connect with it.

I suppose we can't really connect with nothingness, or emptiness. I think that in order for us to advance and be creative as a society we need to be surrounded by art and beauty, and of course, by the people we love. To feel comfortable, to be amongst the things we have collected over our lifetimes is to hold memories close and to feel a connection with the past. For me it creates a feeling of security. Light, objects, memory, and love are the ingredients needed to create such a place. I confess I could never be a monk. I need my house, my things, my art. I need beauty in my life—for a creative person it is vital. These "things" are like talismans collected over time; they are protective and comforting. Of course, I could live without them, and indeed it is often necessary to do so and find inspiration elsewhere; but these elements help me to thrive and to grow. I suppose in some way they echo my past memories and remind me of experiences that collectively amount to a life.

SERENA BASS

Finding Home

AT TWELVE YEARS OLD, I went on a cruise with my aged father and my despised stepmother, who actually did have a wart on the end of her nose. We visited Mediterranean ports and Greek islands, as had been promised. Originally, there was a great deal of excitement about the idea of this holiday, hoping to meet other families with children of my own age. But it was not as imagined, since what we boarded wasn't a real cruise ship, but a cargo boat and we were the only passengers. A ruse (rhymes with cruise, see?) by my father, as my stepmother had asked for the one thing and my father could only afford the other.

Out of the blue I was corralled to play bridge so that, with the captain, we'd be a foursome. The hatred between my stepmother and me became theatrical since the captain was a good teacher and I picked up the concept like a born card shark, who also couldn't stop snorting with delight every time my father and I won a hand.

Once off the boat, it was expected that I stay not just within sight but virtually welded to their sides. Their cautionary voices trailed off and both looked askance, eyes rolling, considering the idea of what could befall an innocent English girl with pink cheeks and lank brown hair. It was obvious their fears of kidnapping were idiotic and I sighed and seethed.

We had visited Cypress, Beirut, Istanbul, and a port in the Black Sea but had never eaten food other than that prepared by the cook on board. We might as well have not left England since the menu was that of a provincial hotel offering egg mayonnaise, coronation chicken, shepherd's pie, and trifle. Quite astonishing, really, as one could be scraping up the last of the custard and look out of a porthole to see the infinitely exotic domes and minarets of the Turkish skyline.

On the island of Lesbos, out of the blue, an elderly couple my stepmother knew vaguely from the last stop we had made suggested I accompany them on a walk to the top of a wooded mountain. Mysteriously, the stepmother encouraged me to go and in truth I was desperate to get away but frowned with confusion as to why they would let me.

My new friends, Ruby and Jim, were talkative, chatting about the flora, fauna, and customs of the island but then they started to flag and decided to sit for a bit and why didn't I just go on by myself to the top. By myself? Couldn't they almost smell the white slave traders waiting around the bend? Well, that thought evaporated in two seconds, and like a greyhound out of the trap, I was gone.

The sandy path became narrow and rocky and the sounds of the town faded away. No more honking horns, no more radios, no more shouts from the dock. Eventually there was nothing but a natural silence. The sap-filled wind bent the branches of the trees, heavy with pine cones. The path tapered off and I clambered through scrub to the summit. There was a rock, positioned perfectly toward the vista, looking out high over the white houses tumbled along the bay; the sea glittered, and the only movement was from the occasional car winding along the coast road. Gulping in the smell of the pine trees again and again till I was dizzy with the freedom of it all, for the first time in my life I relaxed into being absolutely alone.

I stole as much time as I dared, hypnotically stroking the rock, warm and silky like a Weimaraner, until I acquiesced to reality . . . I simply had to go back down. Expecting an earful of "Where exactly have you been?" But was met with nothing but inquiring smiles. Should we go down and have a little bite before returning to the ship? There was a flash of anxiety. Foreign food. Food eaten actually on foreign soil.

In the square, we sat at a wooden table holding paper napkins, sugar lumps, and toothpicks and I was paralyzed. What should I ask for that might not kill me within the hour, as was the constant cry of my stepmother? I asked for water, but my new good friends suggested lemonade. To the heady question, "Would you like something sweet?" I said, "Yes, please," as what English twelve-year-old would resist, but the image of what it could be was a blank canvas.

The lemonade arrived and was a fascination. It was pale yellow, not clear and fizzy, as expected. It had a jagged chunk of ice floating in the glass and a hefty sprig of mint; there was no straw. I took a sip and registered roses, which was simply beyond my comprehension but made me want to never drink anything else again. Staring at the triangle of filo that accompanied it, the layers of pastry sandwiching jade green pistachios and leaking honey, I fell in love with the absolute foreign-ness of it. It meant I wasn't on the ship, I wasn't at school, I wasn't at my father's house. I was completely elsewhere.

"Darling. Darling, can you hear me?" asked Ruby, dragging me from my imaginings.

We arrived back on the ship and I saw my father and stepmother sitting with cups of tea and chocolate digestives . . . they were the foreigners now.

I settled in to wait them out, knowing there was a world of astonishing food out there for me and having tasted the tip of the iceberg, it was clear that food, the eating and the making of it, and the reveling in the understanding of it, was to be my life and that I had unexpectedly found my way home.

STEVEN R. GAMBREL

The staircase leading to the breakfast room
in my Sag Harbor home. One of the most serene
spaces in the house, the calmness helps
me break away from the bustle of the workweek.

PHOTOGRAPH BY ERIK PIASECKI

TERRIE SULTAN

Home Alone (Not Alone)

I N JUNE OF 1985 I moved to New York from San Francisco, leaving behind my new lover, not knowing if we would ever see each other again. Living in New York had been a long-standing goal, but it was difficult to leave a city I had grown to love, and a man I loved even more. My home for six years had been a top-floor apartment on Nob Hill, where each night I was lulled to sleep by the sound of foghorns. The rooms were intimate, separated by sectioned-glass French doors. Aside from the nightly foghorns, it was so quiet I could hear the clock ticking away the hours. It was a cozy respite from the demands of daily life balanced between graduate school and work.

The shift to New York was simultaneously what I expected and not. The transition from a small chambered apartment to being home, alone, in a large, open-plan loft on the corner of Canal and Eldridge Streets took some getting used to. The tone and tenor of the two neighborhoods also could not have been more different. If Nob Hill was emphatically upscale, residential, and slightly hippyish, my new home was located in a down-at-the-heels area on the Lower East Side replete with sidewalk fruit stands, bartering merchants, and occasional drug dealers and streetwalkers. Rather than the misty fog and chilly temperatures that define a San Francisco summer, my arrival in New York coincided with a prolonged heat wave and a sanitation workers' strike. Constant traffic clamor from the sidewalk and street, and the daily machinations of the industrial neighbors above and below me, resonated throughout the loft. I was lonely, alone, without a job, and knew practically no one. I had no place to go, and only myself to keep me company throughout the day. My lifeline was the letters that flew between New York and San Francisco, a writing campaign that became both daily chronicle and interior dialogue.

Applying, interviewing, and waiting for a job and a place for myself in the world took up most of my days, and often twenty-four hours could pass without my leaving the confines of my not-yet home. While letter writing occupied a fair portion of my time, more was spent trying to work out what my new home was going to mean to me—both home as immediate shelter and comfort, and home as a place of agency and accomplishment.

I spent a fair number of mornings and afternoons sitting on the windowsill spying on the neighbors across the street. I was a Hitchcock fan, and while the parallel with *Rear Window* was obvious, I wasn't searching for dramatic intrigue as much as trying to get a purchase on how others occupied their time when home alone. Besides, observing the daily activities of my neighbors was fascinating. There was very little coming and going; from my perch it appeared that, like me, the inhabitants on the north side of Canal Street were also homebound, either by necessity or design. Their observed lives became a narrative thread in my letters, which included my descriptions based on the intermittent observations I made. As it turned out, some were not entirely accurate.

New York only really became truly home ten months later, when the barrage of letters back and forth between our coastal cities finally, definitively, brought us together when my lover moved East. That move, in turn, set off a cascade of peripatetic domicile shifts from Canal Street to Greenwich Village to the Upper West Side and finally Brooklyn, where we remained settled for a few years. I never lived in another situation that allowed for that distanced but oddly intimate relationship I had with the unknown population across Canal Street. Still, New York became home in the broader sense, even though putting down firm roots in a living situation was elusive. It was surprising to us both then that, after four years, we relocated to Washington, DC, as "home" became a quest for a solid career rather than a place of shelter.

August 20

Dear Christopher

God. Already August 20. I've been here almost 2 months. Do you have enough letters over the past weeks to make a small novel?

My latest form of entertainment: spying on the neighbors across the street. The building looks like this:

Every day the action starts on F - when the Hasedich Jews in their black suits, black hats, sidelocks and beards open shop. Lately, with the advent of the high holy days (early September) some of the men are also wearing pray shawls. They all speak Yiddish and make a lot of noise.

Floor E is empty. Looks like it would be a very nice studio for someone - its been empty for a long time according to T. Lots of windows and light, plus it would be highly entertaining for me, as I can look right down into the space.

Floor D, in the first three windows on the left is an "artist" and his girl friend. He begins the day at 8:30 by drinking a beer, smoking a cigarette while leaning out the window onto the overhang, watching alternatively the street, and me watching him. I use "artist" because I never actually see him work, only drink intermitent beers all day long. Next door to him in the MIG window is an older man who sits at the window all day watching the street.

Floor C B - White haired artist and slim, dark-haired girlfriend who both talk on the telephone all day.

Floor B C - hippy looking painter who paints with no clothes on

Floor A - Never see them, but see lights at night. Maybe they just live there.

My career as a museum professional flourished, as did my lover-then-husband's work as an artist. Washington, DC, proved to be surprisingly sympathetic to our ambitions. And home as shelter also became more solid, as we moved from an enormous rental apartment to the first place we owned. But our sense of home also morphed; home became wherever we were together, and it changed often, from Washington to Paris, back to Washington, to Houston, to the Hamptons on the East End of Long Island. What stayed the same was the sense of being home in what we did—our work, our contributions, and our love for each other.

More than fifteen years later, while attending a seminar in Boston, I had the occasion to spend time with an artist I knew, but whom I had not seen in many years, as we both had departed New York for opportunities in other cities. That evening over cocktails, we talked about our early experiences trying to settle in New York, since both of us had ultimately left for different cities for different reasons. I recounted my first few months, home alone, and how I had become attached to my unknown neighbors across the way. Suddenly, she looked at me, quizzically—"That was you?" she said. I returned the favor: "That was you?" It was, it was. We laughed at this strange, unexpected shared experience.

More than ten years after that, I contacted another artist whose work had always intrigued me, asking for a studio visit. He readily agreed and gave me his address. It was the building on Canal Street that had been the object of so much of my attention decades ago. When I arrived, he met me at the front door and took me into his space. He was on Floor B—the same studio my friend had occupied in the 1980s. Full circle. Home has many meanings, but home as memory can be a powerful uniter.

SUZANNE TUCKER

In so many ways, the essence of home is one's own bed. After a hard day at work or a long week of travel, there is nothing more nurturing and comforting than to climb into one's own bed.

Interior designer Suzanne Tucker and Timothy Marks's bedroom in Montecito, California.

PHOTOGRAPH BY ROGER DAVIES

RITA KONIG

I SPEND A LOT OF TIME THINKING about the essence of what makes a home. There is the layering of elements in a room that I find particularly wholesome and welcoming. There are other revolving goals that I seem to be perpetually striving to achieve. My new one is fridge "styling"—there is something about that family fridge! Americans do it especially well—the fridge being so ordered and abundant—that feeling that at a moment's notice you can produce dinner for six and most definitely an exciting snack for a child. Well-stocked and neatly arranged storage cupboards, whether for linens or other dry goods, are similar—and these things, I know, are hangovers I have brought home to England from my time living in New York. American houses are always ready for a storm. I love the basements filled with plastic containers storing all sorts of items, from light bulbs to Thanksgiving decorations. There is that feeling of preparedness that I love and that gives a reassuring sense of "home."

Abundance is key, and I think that is what I find in this illustration, sent to me as a thank-you note by my talented cousin, Vanessa Konig, after a dinner that encompasses so much of this idea. What is all this decoration and fridge-filling for, if not to entertain your friends and family? I love this intimate view of the room, just as I always love the view from the street into a cozy room on a winter's evening. The golden glow of table lamps seen from outside always suggests the warm arms of the home around its inhabitants. The deep sofa to sink into, fire lit, a good smell coming from the kitchen and, even better, a drink in one's hand and *always* a table beside to rest it on.

When I think about what makes a good home, it is always the feeling rather than the look. The last things to come to mind are the fabrics, wallpapers, and paint colors. It is more about the lighting, scent, furniture, pictures, and the abundance of the essentials fairly close to hand—everything in its place and easy to find. This is something that is easily forgotten when decorating a home, and they are the things that are usually the easiest and most fun things for someone to do—whereas the fabrics and colors cause all sorts of anxiety to many.

The main point to all of this is the people in the house—how they feel in it and the noise, spirit, and warmth they bring. At the time of writing this we are in a pandemic and *locked down*. A couple of nights ago, I saw on a friend's Instagram feed a video of a pre-Covid night of her family and friends around a post-dinner kitchen table, fire lit, and everyone singing. That is what it's all about!

I am looking forward to the return of us gathered around the table together, because that is really what says home to me more than anything.

ILLUSTRATION BY VANESSA KONIG

Thank you ♡ Nene (Neme!)

DRINK GIN

lovely supper with Reta + phil 4 November 2015

TIANA WEBB EVANS

Home

When I think of home, I think of a place
Where there's love overflowing

Home embodies our experience as human beings; it is our outer capsule and the anchoring of our being. Conceptually *home* is an identity marker with the ritualistic quality of initiation that goes beyond physicality of structure or pristine appointments. The anchor of home is molded in childhood when the mindscape is malleable like biblical clay.

I wish I was home, I wish I was back there
With the things I've been knowing

As children, home is large even if it is small, wondrous even if it is simple, singularly important in all of its cracks and crevices.

Our experiences in these moments are interpreted as and through only one lens: love.

Many of us have had the experience of returning to Grandma's as a young adult to discover Oz is actually more modest than we anticipated. But then the scent of bread baking in the kitchen, a sweet word of encouragement, a lace tablecloth, the reliable ticking of a grandfather clock, the feel of a floral-patterned velvet sofa, the sight of a wing-back chair, can shrink us back to the moment when that very space seemed grand. These vessels are the spaces from which we give birth to ourselves.

Wind that makes the tall grass bend into leaning
Suddenly the raindrops that fall have a meaning

At home we learn to listen. Our environment becomes our tuner. Whether listening to birdsong or boom boxes in the morning or whistling frogs or sirens in the nighttime, our ears are molded into receptors. We all don't hear the same things; many of us have to be taught to listen.

As a child I had the gift of many homes, in terms of landscape and culture. This unusual variety heightened my senses, and activating these faculties sharply focuses my world. Home was a transient and complicated thing. Luckily I was able to root fully in my grandparents' gracious modernist house in Jamaica. Divine in both order and decor. My grandfather was a real estate developer and my grandmother an aesthete of the highest order. Home for them was a carefully composed orchestra of community, cuisine, fashion, and furniture. There I rooted in their elegant version of life.

Suddenly, my world's gone and changed its face
But still I know where I'm going

On the mainland, things were slightly different; my home life was more like experimental jazz, a beep and a bop, a zig and a zag. With separated parents, additional worlds connected more homes to the center pole of Grandma and Grandpa's house in Kingston, Jamaica. Dallas, Texas, to Port Antonio, Jamaica, and back to Queens, New York.

Cowboys, pickup trucks, country music, steak, singing cicadas, and the smell of the old library defined the first half of my summer while the remote Jamaican countryside claimed the rest. We left Texas with enough suitcases to supply a village's young people with clothing, sweets, and toys for our annual three-week immersion in Jamaica's rawness. A stark juxtaposition to my maternal grandparents' rigid protocols, this was naked abandon. Learning to love the overwhelming wonder of nature and respecting our insignificance in the face of the universe. Finding home in rivers, mountains, puddles, and sand.

And if you're listening, God
Please, don't make it hard

To know if we should believe the things we see
Tell us, should we try and stay
Or should we run away
Or is it better just to let things be?

New York, on the other hand, was full of a different kind of adventure—hustle, bustle, striving, pushing, glamour, with a side dish of strife. Home was defined by the hypnotic energy of chasing the American Dream, not a basic dream, because we already had that where we came from, but the dream of vast riches. When life was stable, the dice was rolled. As the slowing tick-tick-tick of the roll stopped, the rules shifted. A life of corporate-enabled, 1980s middling splendor came to a screeching halt. They didn't quite understand how the game was rigged and that a poorly calculated risk could result in ruin. Our home was lost, literally and figuratively.

Living here in this brand new world
Might be a fantasy

Home has become a central character in my play and has sparked a full immersion into the theory of home, a sense of a place, belonging, and a delight in the most dynamic imaginations of home.

In an attempt to reclaim the sense of security lost in my teenage years, I made a home early. We moved to a metropolitan suburb that feels quite like a fantasy. This community, a village, has coalesced around the shared ideals of providing the best life possible for its children and, in turn, produces children who feel the world is theirs to mold. It is a connected fabric of people empowered with the resources to act on their ideas—people who, together, have committed, despite differences, to the collective good.

Nevertheless, we're not far from a world unaligned with our sense of potential and possibility, where communities are actively disempowered and struggle against the attacks on their humanity and their right to materialize their imagination. Gloria Jean Watkins (known as bell hooks) often talks about the power of imagination as a transformative force that can "spark a spirit of transcendent survival."

How much of our own humanity is lost in both the careless and the willfully constructed disparities of access to food, clothing, and shelter experienced by our brothers and sisters?

We need a home for physical security and reinforcement, as much as we need home to anchor our sense of self. "We require places where the values outside of us encourage and enforce the values within us," says philosopher Alain de Botton. "We depend on our surroundings obliquely to embody the modes and the ideas we respect and then to remind us of them."

And I learned that we must look
Inside our hearts to find
A world full of love
Like yours, like mine
Like home

Together we're tasked with creating a culture that acknowledges and respects interbeing, recognizing home as the seed of life and place as a forceful imprint.

No need for pity.

There is only a need for love.

WENDY ARTIN

*T*HIS PAINTING is of a juicy fig from the Roman market downstairs, nestling within my favorite Moroccan bowl.
I bought the bowl with my husband in a souk in Marrakesh. When I saw this bowl I wanted it so much, I lost all reason. The vendor loved my helplessness, and I love seeing this bowl every day.

I have always brought home treasures: a dried earth ball of tiny worm squiggles collected from a childhood semester in England, a faded wooden wine crate from an abandoned warehouse in France, rocks from beaches, and hand-painted ceramics from all over the Mediterranean.

Some treasures are more fleeting. Summers I did not have to hold the glass of the window to keep it closed as we rattled through the countryside in our hand-me-down car. We would screech to a stop when I spotted a heavily laden fig tree, jump out, eat, and fill our bags with delicious figs, purple and green, to bring back to Rome.

With a heart-shaped pink center, the fig is one of the most intimate of fruits. Home is love and food, memories and treasure.

PIETER ESTERSOHN

A. J. Davis was commissioned in 1842 to design
this Gothic Revival schoolhouse in Rhinebeck,
New York. His patron was Mary Garrettson,
whose mother's Livingston inheritance had built
Wildercliff, the name of their property that
surrounded the school. Now a private residence,
this building encompasses so many qualities
that successfully define what a home is for me:
a deep sense of history that cannot be manufactured
but has to be earned; the theme of education,
learning, and libraries that so inspires me; and the
fact that it stands in my favorite region, in an
area and period where the birth of Landscape Design
was introduced and popularized in America.
Plus, it is charming and humble as hell.

WITOLD RYBCZYNSKI

House and Home

"**A** HOUSE IS NOT A HOME," sang Dionne Warwick in the 1964 Burt Bacharach and Hal David ballad. A year later, the British architecture critic Reyner Banham wittily penned "A Home Is Not a House," an essay that characterized the modern dwelling as a "baroque ensemble of domestic gadgets" that could be stuffed into a variety of unorthodox shelters such as caravans and inflatable bubbles. Absent such offbeat and somewhat reductive speculations, the terms *house* and *home* distinguish between the building and the life it contains, and more broadly between a physical shelter and an emotional one. "Going to my house" is an architectural description. "Going home" refers to a safe haven, a place of one's own, whether it is a house, an apartment, a city, or an entire country. That is why Thomas Wolfe's *You Can't Go Home Again* is such a provocative title.

Old English distinguished *hus* from *hām*. The latter proved to be a particularly fecund word that gave us homestead and homeless, homesick and homebody, home plate and home page. Sayings and expressions abound: Home at last, Home is where the heart is, There's no place like home, Keep the home fires burning, Nothing to write home about, Make yourself at home, A man's home is his castle, and of course, Home sweet home.

Thirty years ago I wrote *Home*, a book about the history of domestic comfort. The title proved challenging for foreign publishers. The German and Swedish editions were not a problem, and I'm not sure about the Chinese and Japanese translations, but it turned out that the range of meanings attached to *home* was distinctive to English and some of its Germanic cognates, and did not exist as a single word in most other languages. The Spanish, Italian, and Brazilian editions of my book were titled *La Casa* and *Casa*; in Polish it was *Dom*, which likewise simply means house. In French, "home" is *chez moi* (my place) or simply *la maison* (house). My Quebec publisher finessed the question and titled the book *Le Confort*. Thomas Wolfe was fortunate to write in English; *You Can't Go to Your House Again* doesn't have the same ring.

Words are functional tools. An oenophile needs a variety of terms to distinguish the aroma, taste, and finish of different varietals, while a casual drinker makes do with "red" and "white." Similarly, a skier has many words to describe different types of snow—fresh, powder, corn, crud, slush—whereas to someone who lives in a place where it only occasionally snows, it's only "white stuff." But speaking and writing are not just a means of communication, they are also forms of thinking—out loud and on the page. We need a new word when we want to describe a new thought or feeling. Sometimes we borrow words from other languages, like *angst* or *brio*; sometimes we invent. Think of how many novel words have accompanied the advent of the Internet: hacker, blog, podcast, tweet.

Centuries ago, northern Europeans needed a new word to describe their particular emotional attachment to their dwellings. Exactly why *home* emerged there and not somewhere else is a bit of a mystery. It might have been an accident of language, or it might have been related to the climate; during cold winters, the house is a refuge, a place to keep warm and cozy (a Scottish word). The emergence of the nuclear family may also have had something to do with it, for the word is wrapped in a rich blanket of associated meanings: security, privacy, well-being, domesticity, and the atmosphere of family life.

"There is nothing like staying at home, for real comfort," wrote Jane Austen in *Emma*. She didn't just mean the comfort of an easy chair beside a cozy fire, although that was a part of it. Real comfort also meant being surrounded by family and familiar objects, pictures and books—your own stuff in your own safe place, apart from the world. Enjoying the intimacy and privacy associated with one's home, that is sweetness, indeed.

CARL VILHELM HOLSØE
WOMAN WITH FRUIT BOWL, 1900–10
OIL ON CANVAS

CONTRIBUTOR BIOGRAPHIES

William Abranowicz is a photographer whose work is in public and private collections throughout the United States and Europe. He is the author of five monographs.

Iris Apfel is a "geriatric starlet," fashion icon, interior designer, visiting professor at the University of Texas, author of *Iris Apfel: Accidental Icon* (2018), and subject of Albert Maysles's Emmy-nominated documentary *Iris*. With her husband, Carl, she cofounded Old World Weavers. A Metropolitan Museum of Art exhibition of Apfel's style, *Rara Avis*, traveled across the country. She will be the recipient, in January 2022, of the Andrée Putman Lifetime Achievement Award.

Marc Appleton is the founding principal of Appleton Partners LLP—Architects, with offices in Santa Monica and Santa Barbara, California. A graduate of Harvard College and the Yale School of Architecture, Appleton has won numerous awards and has written, published, and contributed to many books.

Wendy Artin is a painter whose work is included in several private and public collections, including the Museum of Fine Arts, Boston, and the Boston Public Library. Her work has been featured in *Pratique des Arts*, *American Artist*, *Vanity Fair*, Paris *Vogue*, *Elle*, and the *Boston Globe*.

Amy Astley is the editor in chief of *Architectural Digest* and founding editor of *Teen Vogue*.

Jeffrey Banks is a menswear designer and the author of numerous books, including *Norell* (2018), *Perry Ellis* (2013), *Preppy* (2011), and *Tartan* (2007). Banks has received two Coty Awards, for outstanding menswear and men's furs; the Pratt Award for Design Excellence; and other industry distinctions.

Dan Barber is the chef at and co-owner of Blue Hill in New York and Blue Hill at Stone Barns in Westchester County, and the author of *The Third Plate* (2014). Barber also cofounded Row 7 Seed Company, which brings chefs and plant breeders together to develop new varieties of vegetables and grains.

Anthony S. Barnes is a founder of and principal architect at BarnesVanze Architects. Named a member of the AIA College of Fellows for his contributions to the profession, Barnes also serves on the executive committee of the Institute of Classical Architecture & Art (ICAA) and is a board member of the Leaders of Design Council.

Drew Barrymore is an actress, producer, director, talk-show host, and entrepreneur. A design enthusiast and lover of making homes and spaces, she wants to have beauty all around and create joyful eclectic living.

Serena Bass is an executive chef and the author of *Serena, Food & Stories* (2004), which won the James Beard Award for best entertaining book in 2005.

Alex Beard is a painter and the author and illustrator of the storybook series *Tales from the Watering Hole* (2008, 2009, 2010, and 2018). Beard has exhibited extensively throughout the United States, including solo shows in New York, Los Angeles, and New Orleans, and abroad in Hong Kong.

Jamie Beck is a photographer who has collaborated with Chanel, Armani, Oscar de la Renta, and other fashion brands. Her work has been exhibited at the International Center of Photography.

Nicholas Benson is a third-generation stone carver, specializing in architectural lettering for public buildings, memorials, and monuments across the country, including notable civic memorials in Washington, DC. Benson was awarded a MacArthur Fellowship in 2010, which allowed him to explore a thread of artistic work he continues to develop today.

Candice Bergen is an actress, who has won five Emmy and two Golden Globe awards for her work on *Murphy Brown*. In 2016, Bergen launched Bergenbags, an enterprise for which she personally paints images on designer handbags.

Nate Berkus established his interior design firm at age twenty-four. Berkus is included on *Elle Decor*'s A-List and was named to *Architectural Digest*'s AD100 in 2018. His television career has spanned over 150 makeovers on the *Oprah Winfrey Show*, as well as shows on TLC and HGTV.

Michael Boodro is a writer and the former editor in chief of *Elle Decor*. He is host of the *Chairish Podcast* and serves as an advisor to the Design Leadership Network.

Leslie Greene Bowman is president of the Thomas Jefferson Foundation, which owns and operates the UNESCO World Heritage Site, Monticello—the home of Thomas Jefferson—in Charlottesville, Virginia.

David G. Bradley is chairman emeritus of Atlantic Media and chairman of National Journal Group, both publishing companies based in Washington, DC. Bradley's board memberships include Swarthmore College, American University of Beirut, KIPP DC, and the Child Protection Network. He is a member of the Council on Foreign Relations and the American Academy of Arts and Sciences.

Melissa Biggs Bradley is the founder and chief executive officer of travel-planning company Indagare, which has been named to the Inc. 5000 and Crain's Fast 50 lists, in recognition of its being one of the fastest-growing companies in the United Sates.

Jeremiah Brent founded his interior design firm in 2011 and has established himself as both a taste-maker and influencer through various partnerships, television series, and branded collaborations. Brent has been featured in publications such as *Domino*, *Architectural Digest*, and *Harper's Bazaar*.

Joan Juliet Buck is the author of two novels and an acclaimed memoir, *The Price of Illusion* (2017). Her 2020 online diary was anthologized by *StatORec* magazine in *Writing the Virus*, and nominated for a Pushcart Prize. An American from Paris and London and longtime contributing editor to *Vogue* and *Vanity Fair*, Buck was editor in chief of Paris *Vogue* for seven years.

Martyn Lawrence Bullard is a Los Angeles–based interior designer known for his broad range of styles and inviting interiors. Consistently named to *Architectural Digest*'s AD100, Bullard has collaborated with Ann Sacks, The Rug Company, and Corbett Lighting. His celebrity clients include Kylie Jenner, Cher, and Tommy Hilfiger.

Tory Burch is the executive chairman and chief creative officer of Tory Burch LLC, an American luxury brand. In 2009, she launched the Tory Burch Foundation to advance women's empowerment and entrepreneurship in the United States. She has been named to *Forbes* magazine's The World's 100 Most Powerful Women and *Glamour*'s Women of the Year.

Christy Turlington Burns is a global maternal health advocate and founder of Every Mother Counts, a nonprofit organization committed to making pregnancy and childbirth safe for every mother, everywhere. For this work, she was recognized as one of *Time* magazine's Time 100, a list of the most influential people in the world. Burns is also an author, filmmaker, and model.

Nina Campbell is an interior designer, renowned for her contagious wit and sense of style. Her designs appeal to both young and old and sit well in both contemporary and traditional interiors. Nina has a fabric and wallpaper collection sold worldwide, has a furniture and home accessories line, and has written a number of books on interior design.

Addie Chapin is an artist whose work is displayed in commercial and private collections in New York, Atlanta, Nashville, and beyond.

Debra Martin Chase is a trailblazing producer and chief executive officer of Martin Chase Productions. Her work has garnered Academy Award, Emmy Award, NAACP Image Award, and Peabody Award nominations. Chase serves on the boards of the New York City Ballet and the Second Stage Theater in Manhattan.

Lena Ciardullo is the executive chef at New York's Union Square Cafe. She was previously executive chef at Marta, Caffe Marchio, and Vini e Fritti, Union Square Hospitality Group's Roman-inspired restaurants.

William Curtis is an architect and a founding principal of Curtis & Windham Architects. He has received numerous honors, including the ICAA's Arthur Ross Award and is the author of the monograph *A Vision of Place* (2016).

John Derian is an artist and designer of decoupage pieces, ephemera, ceramics, and furniture. In 1989, he established John Derian Company Inc. His work and homes have been featured in *Vogue*, *The New York Times*, *The World of Interiors*, *Elle Decor*, and *Vanity Fair*. *The John Derian Picture Book* (2016) is a *New York Times* best seller.

Dimorestudio was founded in Milan in 2003 by Britt Moran and Emiliano Salci as a full-service, global architectural and design firm that encompasses residential, retail, and hospitality projects, in addition to producing furnishings, textiles, and lighting designs.

Stan Dixon is an architect and founder of D. Stanley Dixon Architect, Inc. He has received the Southeast Architect of the Year award by *Veranda* magazine and the Atlanta Decorative Arts Center, the Philip Trammell Shutze Award by the ICAA, and the Addison Mizner Medal for his work in Palm Beach.

Jamie Drake is an interior designer and cofounder of Drake/Anderson. He is a member of *Elle Decor*'s A-List and *Architectural Digest*'s AD100. His numerous industry honors include Fashion Group International's Night of Stars award for interior design, the ASID College of Fellows, and *Interior Design* magazine's Interior Design Hall of Fame.

Jeffrey Dungan is an award-winning architect whose work has been featured in *Architectural Digest*, *Milieu*, *Veranda*, the *Wall Street Journal*, *Luxe Interiors + Design*, *Garden & Gun*, and other publications. His book, *The Nature of Home* (2018), is in its seventh printing. Dungan's projects span the United States, Costa Rica, and Nova Scotia.

Craig Dykers, FAIA, Int FRIBA, FRSA, RAAR, is an architect and founding partner of the international design practice Snøhetta. The studio focuses on well-being, biodiversity, sustainability, and empowering communities. Dykers's work is recognized for promoting social diversity and environmental responsibility that positively impacts cities, habitats, and people.

Emily Evans Eerdmans is a design historian, gallery owner, and author of several books, including *Henri Samuel: Master of the French Interior* (2018), *Mario Buatta: Fifty Years of American Interior Decoration* (2013), *The World of Madeleine Castaing* (2010), and the 1958–2012 catalogue raisonné of furniture artist Wendell Castle (2013).

Pieter Estersohn is a photographer and author. His latest book, *Life Along the Hudson* (2018), came about through his curiosity as president of the Friends of Clermont. His next book with Rizzoli will document the new wave in agriculture in New York's Hudson River Valley. Estersohn is organizing a symposium on nineteenth-century landscape with The Calvert Vaux Preservation Alliance.

Tiana Webb Evans is the founder of ESP Group—a brand strategy and communications agency focused on the art and design industries, the founder and creative director of Yard Concept, and the founding director of Jamaica Art Society. She writes about culture, advises and supports emerging artists, and serves on the boards of Project for Empty Space and the Female Design Council.

Julian Fellowes is a screenwriter, actor, novelist, film director, and a Conservative peer in the House of Lords.

Pamela Fiori was editor in chief of both *Travel + Leisure* and *Town & Country*. Since retirement from Hearst, Fiori has authored and contributed to numerous books on travel and social history, including *Holiday: The Best Travel Magazine that Ever Was* (2019).

Miguel Flores-Vianna is an editor, writer, and photographer. He is the author of *A Wandering Eye: Travels with My Phone* (2019) and *Haute Bohemians* (2017).

Douglas Friedman is a photographer, specializing in architecture, design, fashion, and portraiture. His work has been featured in *Architectural Digest*, *Wallpaper*, *Elle Decor*, *Harper's Bazaar*, and *Vanity Fair*.

Ken Fulk is an interior designer known for his layered interiors, historic restorations, clever brand identities, and unforgettable parties. Twice nominated for James Beard Design Awards, Fulk's hospitality projects have gained him notoriety as a destination-maker for hotels, restaurants, and private social clubs. He is included on *Architectural Digest*'s AD100 and *Elle Decor*'s A-List.

Steven R. Gambrel is the founder and president of the interior design firm S.R. Gambrel, Inc. and the author of *Steven Gambrel: Perspective* (2018) and *Steven Gambrel: Time and Place* (2012). His firm's work has been featured in *The World of Interiors*, *Architectural Digest*, *House & Garden*, *Town & Country*, *House Beautiful*, *New York* magazine, *The New York Times*, and *Elle Decor*.

Zoltan Gerliczki is a filmmaker, painter, computer artist, and graphic designer. As a postproduction artist, he has worked on projects with various publications, including *Elle Decor*, *House Beautiful*, and *Travel + Leisure*. Gerliczki's work has been exhibited worldwide at museums and galleries.

Oberto Gili is a photographer who specializes in interiors and fashion. The author of *Domus* (2016) and *Home Sweet Home* (2011), he works for such publications as the *Wall Street Journal*, *Architectural Digest*, *Travel + Leisure*, and *Vogue*.

Seth Godin is the author of twenty best-selling books that have been translated into thirty-five languages. In addition to writing the most popular marketing blog in the world, he is the founder of altMBA, the former vice president of direct marketing at Yahoo!, and a five-time TED speaker.

Wendy Goodman is the design editor of *New York* magazine. She is the author of *May I Come In? Discovering the World in Other People's Houses* (2018) and *The World of Gloria Vanderbilt* (2010), as well as the coauthor of *Tony Duquette* (2007).

Renée and John Grisham live in an old Virginia house dating back two hundred years, where he writes every day and she manages the family foundation and also serves on the Share Our Strength board.

Hugo Guinness is a painter, illustrator, and writer. His work has been featured in such publications as *The New York Times*, *The New Yorker*, and *Vogue*. With Wes Anderson, Guinness shares an Oscar nomination for the *Grand Budapest Hotel* screenplay. His work is available at John Derian and on his website.

Dayle Haddon is a spokesperson, activist, author, and fashion model. Haddon is a UNICEF Ambassador and founder of WomenOne, a charitable organization focused on the quality education of girls and women around the world.

Michael Hainey is a writer, editor, and artist. The deputy editor of *Air Mail*, he formerly worked at *GQ* and *Esquire*. Hainey is also the author of the best-selling memoir *After Visiting Friends* (2013).

Kitty Hawks is an interior designer who has taught traditional residential interior design at the Parsons School of Design. She was inducted into the *Interior Design* Hall of Fame in 2005.

Michael Imber is the principal architect of Michael G. Imber, Architects, PLLC, a modern classical design firm based in San Antonio, Texas. Imber has been honored with numerous design awards, notably the Arthur Ross Award (ICAA) for lifetime achievement.

Gabriella Imperatori-Penn is a still-life and interior design photographer. Her fine art work is held in numerous private collections and has been shown by Steven Kasher Gallery, Exhibit A London, Rhode Island Center for Photographic Arts, and Space Gallery in St. Barth and New York City.

Pamela Jaccarino is an artist and, since 2005, the founding editor in chief of *Luxe Interiors + Design*, the largest architecture and design brand in the country. Jaccarino was an executive editor with the LVMH Group.

Bianca Jagger is a human rights and environment defender. She is the founder and president of the Bianca Jagger Human Rights Foundation, Council of Europe goodwill ambassador, member of the executive director's leadership council of Amnesty International USA, and a former actress.

Corey Damen Jenkins is an interior designer. His work has been published in *House Beautiful* and *Traditional Home*. In 2020 he was named to *Elle Decor*'s A-List, and in 2021 he was inducted into *Architectural Digest*'s AD100. Jenkins has appeared as a design expert on HGTV and *Rachael Ray*.

Jill Kargman is an author, writer, and actress. Her books include *Sprinkle Glitter on my Grave* (2016) and *Momzillas* (2007), which was adapted into the Bravo television show *Odd Mom Out*.

Eleanora Kennedy is an interior designer, writer, and courtroom consultant. She has contributed to numerous magazines, including *Hamptons Cottages & Gardens* where she served as editor at large. Kennedy is a board member of the Society of Memorial Sloan Kettering Cancer Center, codirector of the Shana Alexander Charitable Foundation, and board member of the Central Park Conservancy.

Delia Kenza is an interior designer who specializes in complete renovations of urban living spaces. Her work has been featured in *New York* magazine, *Dwell*, *House Beautiful*, and *Brownstoner*, as well as on HGTV and during Open House New York.

Chip Kidd is a graphic designer and author known for his book covers and graphic novels. Kidd has received the AIGA Medal, the National Design Award for Communication Design, and the International Center of Photography's Infinity Award for the use of photography in design.

Thomas A. Kligerman is an architect and cofounder of Ike Kligerman Barkley. He graduated with a Bachelor of Arts from Columbia University and a Master of Architecture from Yale School of Architecture. He serves on the boards of a number of charitable and educational institutions.

Rita Konig is an interior designer and principal of her own interior design studio. Based in London, the firm works on residential and commercial projects in London, New York, Nashville, and California, including decorating Los Angeles's most sought-after new members' club, the San Vicente Bungalows.

Larry Lederman is a retired corporate lawyer and landscape photographer. His work has been published in six books, including *Garden Portraits* (2020) and *Interior Landmarks: Treasures of New York* (2018). Lederman's work is held by numerous corporate and private collections, including The New York Botanical Garden, Montefiore Hospital, The New York School of Interior Design, and Winterthur.

Annie Leibovitz is a photographer, who has been designated a Living Legend by the Library of Congress and is the recipient of many other honors. Her work has been exhibited in museums worldwide, including the National Portrait Gallery in Washington, DC, the International Center of Photography in New York, the Maison Européene de la Photographie in Paris, and the Hermitage Museum, St. Petersburg, Russia.

Kinsey Marable is a private library curator and a bookseller, dealing in rare and out-of-print books. His clients, from around the world, include Tory Burch, Donna Karan, and Oprah Winfrey.

Steele Thomas Marcoux is editor in chief of *Veranda*. She has a twelve-plus-year career of editorial roles at *Southern Living*, *Cottage Living*, *Coastal Living*, and *Country Living*.

Kelly Marshall is a photographer specializing in interiors, food, and portraiture. She is a regular contributor to the *Wall Street Journal* and *Architectural Digest*. Marshall's work has been exhibited at Photoville, MOAD: The Museum of The African Diaspora, Southern Exposure, and Rush Arts Gallery.

Kim McCarty is a painter who resides in Los Angeles. Her work is in private and public collections, including the Hammer Museum of Art in Los Angeles and The Museum of Modern Art in New York.

Marian McEvoy is the former European editor of *Women's Wear Daily* and *W* magazine, editor in chief of *Elle Decor*, and editor in chief of *House Beautiful*.

Jon Meacham is a writer, reviewer, historian, and presidential biographer. A former executive editor and executive vice president at Random House, he is a contributing writer to *The New York Times Book Review*, a contributing editor to *Time* magazine, and a former editor in chief of *Newsweek*.

Danny Meyer is the founder and chief executive officer of Union Square Hospitality Group, which has created some of New York's most beloved restaurants, cafes, and bars. Meyer cowrote *The Union Square Cafe Cookbook* (1994), which earned the Julia Child Award (International Association of Culinary Professionals), and contributed to several subsequent books. Meyer sits on the boards of Share Our Strength, City Harvest, The Madison Square Park Conservancy, and other organizations.

Doug Meyer is an artist and designer based in New York City, whose work ranges from site-specific spaces to three-dimensional pieces. He is the author of *Heroes: A Tribute* (2019).

Bette Midler is a singer, actress, author, and philanthropist. She has received many awards including four Grammy Awards, three Emmy Awards, two Tony Awards, and three Golden Globe Awards. Midler is the founder of the New York Restoration Project, an open space conservancy and New York City's largest private land trust.

Isaac Mizrahi is a fashion designer, author, television presenter, and chief designer of the Isaac Mizrahi collection for Xcel Brands. He has made countless appearances in movies and on television.

Martina Mondadori, born in Milan where she acquired an early passion for art and connoisseurship from her parents, is a cofounder and editor in chief of *Cabana* magazine, and the European editor at large for *Town & Country*. Earlier in her career, she ran a creative agency in Milan and started the semiannual fashion magazine *Anew*. She authored *The Interiors and Architecture of Renzo Mongiardino* (2017).

Deborah Needleman is a writer, craftsperson, and consultant who was previously editor in chief of *T: The New York Times Style Magazine* and *WSJ*, and founder of *Domino* magazine.

David Netto is an interior designer and writer. His projects have been published in *Vogue*, *Elle Decor*, *House Beautiful*, *House & Garden*, and *Veranda*, as well as several books. Netto worked as contributing design editor to the *Wall Street Journal* and *T: The New York Times Style Magazine*, and writes a column for *Town & Country*. He authored *François Catroux* (2016) and is currently working on a book about Stephen Sills.

Rose Noel is the executive chef of Maialino Mare in Washington, DC, Union Square Hospitality Group's Roman-style trattoria and the coastal sister to the original Maialino, located in New York's Gramercy Park Hotel.

Joyce Carol Oates, a member of the American Academy of Arts and Letters since 1978, is the author most recently of the novel *Breathe* (2021) and the story collection *Night, Neon* (2021). The 2019 recipient of the Jerusalem Prize and the 2020 recipient of the Cino Del Duca Award for World Literature, she teaches at Princeton and New York University.

Michael James O'Brien is a photographer and published poet whose work has been featured in *The New Yorker*, *Rolling Stone*, *GQ UK*, *The New York Times Magazine*, *New York* magazine, British *Vogue*, *L'Uomo Vogue*, *Elle Decor*, *Departures*, *Travel + Leisure*, and more. O'Brien's pieces are included in the permanent collections of the National Portrait Gallery, London; Cleveland Museum of Art; and Joyce Holdings in Beijing.

Enuma Okoro is a Nigerian-American writer, speaker, and cultural curator. A weekend columnist for the *Financial Times*, she has authored books of nonfiction, as well as articles and essays for *The New York Times*, *Aeon*, *Artsy*, *Harper's Bazaar*, *Cultured*, *Vogue*, *The Atlantic*, *The Guardian*, *The Washington Post*, *Essence*, and more.

Duro Olowu is a Nigerian-born British fashion designer and curator who has received numerous accolades, including the New Designer of the Year Award at the British Fashion Awards. Exhibitions curated by him include *Making & Unmaking* (2016) at the Camden Arts Centre in London and *Duro Olowu: Seeing Chicago* at the Museum of Contemporary Art in Chicago.

Mitchell Owens is a writer, editor, and former decorative arts editor of *Architectural Digest*. He is the author of numerous design books, including *Fabulous! The Dazzling Interiors of Tom Britt* (2017) and *In House* (2009).

Umberto Pasti is a writer, horticulturalist, and collector. He is the author of several books including *The Age of Flowers* (2000).

Irving Penn was an American photographer known for his fashion photography, portraits, and still lifes. Penn was celebrated as one of *Vogue* magazine's top photographers for more than sixty years.

Alexandra Penney is an artist, author, former editor in chief of *Self* magazine, and the originator of the Pink Ribbon for breast cancer awareness. She is the author of many best sellers, including *The Bag Lady Papers* (2010), and has had numerous solo photography exhibitions in New York, Berlin, and Miami Beach at Art Basel.

Clare Potter is a ceramic artist. She has had a number of exhibitions, including shows at Emmanuel Moatti Gallery in Paris and Mallett in New York and London. Her work has been featured in the windows of Tiffany & Co. in New York.

David Prior is cofounder and chief executive officer of PRIOR, former contributing international editor of *Condé Nast Traveler*, and former contributing editor at *Vogue Living*.

Caroline Lee Radziwill, also known as Princess Lee Radziwill, was an American socialite and interior decorator. She was the younger sister of First Lady Jacqueline Bouvier Kennedy and sister-in-law of President John F. Kennedy. Radziwill was known for her sharp, unerring eye and elegant, easy style.

Rachael Ray is a television personality, businesswoman, celebrity cook, philanthropist, and author. She hosts the Emmy Award–winning daytime talk show *Rachael Ray* and the Food Network series *30 Minute Meals*. In 2007, Ray launched the nonprofit Yum-o!, which empowers kids and their families to develop healthy relationships with food and cooking. She has lines of kitchen items, home furnishings, and pet food, Rachael Ray Nutrish.

Julia Reed was a journalist, author, and a contributing editor at *Vogue* and *Newsweek*. She authored numerous books including *Julia Reed's New Orleans* (2019), *South Toward Home* (2018), and *But Mama Always Put Vodka in Her Sangria!* (2014).

Donald Robertson is an artist and a creative director for Esteé Lauder Companies. He is the author of *Donald: The Book* (2017) and children's books *Mitford at the Hollywood Zoo* (2017) and *Mitford at the Fashion Zoo* (2015).

Al Roker is the Emmy Award–winning weatherman for NBC's *Today*. In his forty-year career he has also taken on the roles of journalist, television personality, actor, and book author.

Michael J. Rosen is an author, illustrator, and editor of over one hundred fifty books. He works as a James Thurber scholar, painter, sculptor, and poet. In addition, he has edited seven books to profit Share Our Strength during his fourteen years as a member of its national board of directors. He has received numerous distinctions, including the National Jewish Book Award and Share Our Strength's lifetime achievement award.

Robert Rufino is the style director at *House Beautiful*. He spent the last decade in similar roles at other top-tier design magazines, such as *Elle Decor* and *Architectural Digest*. Earlier in his career, Rufino was vice president of creative services and visual merchandising at Tiffany & Co. and visual planning director at Henri Bendel.

Witold Rybczynski is an architect and professor emeritus at the University of Pennsylvania. He studied architecture at McGill University in Montreal where he also taught. He has been an architecture critic for *Slate* and is the author of more than twenty books, including a prize-winning biography of Frederick Law Olmsted.

Charles Dare Scheips is a painter, curator, art advisor, and cultural historian. He is the author of *Elsie de Wolfe's Paris: Frivolity Before the Storm* (2014), *American Fashion* (2007), and *Andy Warhol: The Day the Factory Died* (2006). Scheips's writing has appeared in numerous publications, including *Harper's Bazaar, Vogue, Vanity Fair,* and *Architectural Digest*. He is represented by the Richard Taittinger Gallery in New York.

Annie Schlechter is a photographer. Her clients include *House Beautiful, New York* magazine, *Better Homes & Gardens, Veranda, Condé Nast Traveler,* and *The World of Interiors*. Schlechter has contributed to many interior design books and cookbooks, including *New York Behind Closed Doors* (2017) by Polly Devlin and *Carne* (2016) by Christopher Behr.

Edwin Schlossberg is a designer, author, and artist. He is the author of eleven books, including *Einstein and Beckett* (1973). His artwork has been presented in many one-man shows and museum exhibitions. Schlossberg has received many honors, including his appointment to the US Commission of Fine Arts by President Barack Obama.

Susie Orman Schnall is the author of four novels: *We Came Here to Shine* (2020), *The Subway Girls* (2018), *The Balance Project* (2015), and *On Grace* (2014). Her articles have appeared in numerous publications, including *The New York Times, The Huffington Post, PopSugar, Writer's Digest,* and *Glamour*. Schnall is a frequent speaker on her novels and work-life balance, at women's groups, corporations, and book clubs.

Marie-Louise Sciò is the chief executive officer and creative director of Pellican Hotels and president and creative director of the Pellicano Group. Sciò's family, which has owned and operated the Hotel Il Pellicano in Porto Ercole, Italy, since 1979, also owns La Posta Vecchia and the Mezzatorre hotels.

Margot Shaw is the founder and editor in chief of *Flower* magazine. She is on the national advisory committees of the Antiques & Garden Show of Nashville and the Lauritzen Gardens Antiques Show in Omaha, as well as a board member of the Antiques at the Gardens in Birmingham. Shaw authored *Living Floral: Entertaining and Decorating with Flowers* (2019) and is on the advisory board for the Depression & Suicide Center at the University of Alabama at Birmingham.

Jim Shepard is the author of eight novels, including most recently *Phase Six* (2021) and *The Book of Aron* (2015), which won the Sophie Brody Medal for Achievement in Jewish Literature from the American Library Association and the PEN/New England Award for fiction. He teaches at Williams College.

Debra Shriver is a photographer and writer who has authored three books on New Orleans and one on Paris. She is founder of Crescent City Press, a publishing imprint based in New Orleans.

Fanny Singer is a writer, art critic, and cofounder of the design brand Permanent Collection. Her writing has appeared in *Artforum, Frieze, WSJ, T: The New York Times Style Magazine*, and other publications. Singer is the author of *Always Home: A Daughter's Recipes & Stories* (2020).

Hunt Slonem is a fine artist who is best known for his series of bunnies, butterflies, and tropical birds, as well as his large-scale sculptures and restorations of forgotten historical houses. Slonem's works can be found in the permanent collections of museums around the world, including the Solomon R. Guggenheim Museum, the Metropolitan Museum of Art, and the New Orleans Museum of Art.

Clinton Smith is a New York–based editor, designer, and author. He has written four books—on flowers, entertaining, decorating with color, and outdoor living—and currently serves as editor at large for *New England Home* and style editor at *Atlanta Homes & Lifestyles*. Smith previously served as the editor in chief of *Veranda*.

Matthew Patrick Smyth is an interior designer consistently listed on *Elle Decor*'s A-List. His work has appeared in *House Beautiful, Traditional Home, New York* magazine, *Architectural Digest, The New York Times*, and *Flower* magazine. Smyth is a recipient of the D&D Building's Stars of Design Award.

Andrew Solomon, author of *Far from the Tree* (2012) and *The Noonday Demon* (2001), is a writer and lecturer on politics, culture, and psychology; winner of the National Book Award; and an activist for LGBTQ rights, mental health, and the arts. He is professor of clinical medical psychology (in psychiatry) at Columbia University Medical Center and a former president of PEN America Center.

Gloria Steinem is a writer, political activist, and feminist organizer. She is a founder of *New York* and *Ms.* magazines and has authored many books. Steinem cofounded the National Women's Political Caucus, the Ms. Foundation for Women, the Free to Be Foundation, and the Women's Media Center.

Terrie Sultan is an independent curator and cultural consultant. She is the former director of the Parrish Art Museum in Water Mill, New York, where she served for twelve years. Prior to that position, Sultan was director of the Blaffer Art Museum at the University of Houston.

Keith Summerour is an architect and founder of the firm Summerour Architects. His work has been featured in *Architectural Digest, Garden & Gun*, and *Coastal Living*. The firm has published two monographs: *Creating Home: Design for Living* (2017) and *Summerour: Architecture of Permanence, Scale, and Proportion* (2006).

John Charles Thomas is an attorney and retired justice of the Supreme Court of Virginia.

Ruben Toledo is an artist and designer who has illustrated many books and contributed to numerous magazines. Collaborations with his late wife, fashion designer Isabel Toledo, have been exhibited at the Museum at FIT in New York, Columbus Museum of Art, the Detroit Institute of Arts, and others.

Suzanne Tucker is an interior designer. She has been included in *Architectural Digest*'s AD100 numerous times, and her work has been featured in design magazines around the world. She has authored *Suzanne Tucker Interiors: The Romance of Design* (2013) and *Rooms to Remember: The Classic Interiors of Suzanne Tucker* (2009).

Clarissa Ward is CNN's award-winning chief international correspondent. For more than fifteen years, Ward has reported from front lines across the world and received two Emmys for her work. She is the author of *On All Fronts: The Education of a Journalist* (2020).

Alice Waters is a chef, author, food activist, and the founder and owner of Chez Panisse restaurant in Berkeley, California. In 1995, she founded The Edible Schoolyard Project to transform the health of children by designing hands-on educational experiences in the garden, kitchen, and cafeteria that teaches them critical thinking around food and connects them to nature, and to each other. She has received numerous awards, including the National Humanities Medal from President Obama in 2014.

Simon Watson, a native of Dublin, is an interiors photographer whose work appears in such periodicals as *T: The New York Times Style Magazine, W* magazine, *Travel + Leisure*, and *Vanity Fair*. He photographs for major print advertising and catalog campaigns and authored *The Lives of Others* (2020), a monograph of his interiors and portraits. His photography is included in museum, public, private, and corporate collections in the United States and Europe.

Kelly Wearstler is founder and principal of Kelly Wearstler Interior Design. The American designer is a celebrated member of the AD100 Hall of Fame and listed in *Time* magazine's Design 100. Wearstler has authored four monographs, including *Kelly Wearstler: Evocative Style* (2019), and is the first interior designer to teach a MasterClass (2020).

Caroline Weber is a French literature professor at Barnard and Columbia; she is also currently a Guggenheim Fellow and a Fellow at the New York Public Library's Cullman Center. Her latest book, *Proust's Duchess* (2018), was a finalist for the Pulitzer Prize in biography.

Claudia Weill is a film, television, and theater director. Her feature film, *Girlfriends* (1978), was recently acquired by the Criterion Collection and honored by being included in the National Film Archive of the Library of Congress. Weill has directed episodic television (*My So Called Life, thirtysomething*, and *Girls*) and teaches extensively.

Hutton Wilkinson is an interior designer, jewelry designer, and author. As creative director and president of Tony Duquette Inc., he licenses original designs for textiles, lighting, carpets, furniture, and accessories around the world. Wilkinson is the president of the Duquette Foundation for the Living Arts and the Elsie de Wolfe Foundation.

Susan Wissler is executive director of The Mount, Edith Wharton's home in Lenox, Massachusetts.

Ann Ziff is chairman of the Metropolitan Opera and vice chairman of Lincoln Center for the Performing Arts. She is also vice chairman of the Artist Tribe Foundation. She currently serves on several boards including the Los Angeles Opera Company, LACMA, and the New York Restoration Project. Ziff was awarded an Honorary Doctorate in Humane Letters from the Juilliard School and an Honorary Doctorate in Humanities from Wittenberg University. Ms. Ziff designs and makes jewelry for her own company Tamsen Z.

DONORS

No Kid Hungry extends its sincere appreciation to the supporters of *Home*.

Project Chairs
Charlotte Moss | Rizzoli International Publications

Vice Chairs
Anthony S. Barnes | Michael Imber | Thomas A. Kligerman

No Kid Hungry Champions
Philip and Vanina Grovit
Mary Solomon

School Breakfast Leaders
Anonymous in honor of Charlotte Moss
Candace and Rick Beinecke
Michele and Marty Cohen
Leah and Alain Lebec
Julie and Brian Simmons
Diane and Tom Tuft

Hunger Heroes
Peggy and Keith Anderson
Ronda and Mark Axelowitz
Kristin Kennedy Clark
Curtis & Windham Architects, Inc.
James and Beatrice Del Favero
Lisa Fine
Mary and Jay Flaherty
Hollis and Jim Forbes
Amy and Sid Goodfriend
Andi and Jim Gordon
Suzanne Kasler
Ellen and Howard Katz
Eleanora Kennedy
Brian Lee and Louise Hochberg
Winnie Lerner
Anik and Stephane Levy
Carol and Earle I. Mack
Ann Merck, Ann Long Fine Art
Whitney and Clarke Murphy
Zibby and Kyle Owens
John and Louisa Troubh
Mary Margaret and John Trousdale
Jane and Matthew Tucker
Madeline Weinrib and Graham Head
Beth and John Werwaiss

Supporters
Anonymous
Cathie Black
Taylor Gibson-Ullman
Michelle Lin Greenip
Stan Heilbronn and Wendy Capeluto
Tondra and Jeffrey Lynford
Abby and Howard Milstein
Liz Robbins
Susan Hull Walker and Trenholm Walker
Louis S. and Sarah G. Wolfe

ADDITIONAL CREDITS:

28: © 2020 Ray Marks Co. LLC. All rights reserved.
34: © 2016 Robert Frost Copyright Trust
48: Jeff Hirsch / New York Social Diary
74, 75: © New York Restoration Project
87: Keith Major / Contour by Getty Images
90: Scott Frances / OTTO
99, top row: Silvia Rivoltella, Andrea Ferrari, Silvia Rivoltella, and
    Emanuele Zamponi
99, middle row: Emanuele Zamponi (above), Silvia Rivoltella (below),
    Andrea Ferrari, Andrea Ferrari, and Silvia Rivoltella
99, bottom row: Andrea Ferrari, Danilo Scarpati, Andrea Ferrari, and
    Danilo Scarpati
117: Stephen Kent Johnson / OTTO
126–7: Irving Penn, *Vogue* © Condé Nast
156: Photograph by Miguel Flores-Vianna. Courtesy of *Cabana* magazine.
157: Photograph by Guido Taroni. Courtesy of *Cabana* magazine.
188: © 2021 The Richard Avedon Foundation
213: Museo Nacional Thyssen-Bornemisza / Scala / Art Resource, NY

First published in the United States of America in 2021 by
Rizzoli International Publications, Inc.
300 Park Avenue South
New York, New York 10010
www.rizzoliusa.com

PUBLISHER: Charles Miers
SENIOR EDITOR: Philip Reeser
PRODUCTION MANAGER: Alyn Evans
DESIGN COORDINATOR: Olivia Russin
COPY EDITOR: Victoria Brown
PROOFREADER: Sarah Stump
MANAGING EDITOR: Lynn Scrabis

PROJECT MANAGER: Kimberly Power

DESIGNER: Aaron Garza

ISBN: 978-0-8478-7090-5
Library of Congress Control Number: 2021933878

2021 2022 2023 2024 / 10 9 8 7 6 5 4 3 2 1

PRINTED AND BOUND IN ITALY

Facebook.com/RizzoliNewYork
Twitter: @Rizzoli_Books
Instagram.com/RizzoliBooks
Pinterest.com/RizzoliBooks
Youtube.com/user/RizzoliNY
Issuu.com/Rizzoli